People and Places in the Texas Past

by June Rayfield Welch

Dallas •  • 1974

YELLOW
R·O·S·E
P·R·E·S·S

Library of Congress Catalog Card No.
74-19747

ISBN 0-912854-05-7

First Printing Sept. 1974
Second Printing Dec. 1975
Third Printing Mar. 1978
Fourth Printing Sept. 1980
Fifth Printing Oct. 1987

Published by

Dallas, Texas

Printed
by

Waco, Texas

To the memory of my father, the best man I ever knew.

Frank Albert Welch, born 5 July 1904 in the Chickasaw Nation, Indian Territory, died 14 March 1987 at Brownwood, Texas. (His good buddy here is great-granddaughter Melissa McBride Mundorf.)

Books by June Rayfield Welch

The Texas Courthouse Revisited—1984

A Texan's Garden of Trivia—1984

Riding Fence—1983

The Colleges of Texas—1981

All Hail the Mighty State—1979

The Texas Senator—1978

The Texas Governor—1977

Going Great in the Lone Star State—1976

And Here's to Charley Boyd—1975

The Glory that was Texas—1975

People and Places in Texas Past—1974

Dave's Tune—1973

Historic Sites of Texas—1972

The Texas Courthouse—1971

Texas: New Perspectives—1971

A Family History—1966

Introduction

For anyone with an interest in history Gainesville was not a bad place to grow up, and the depression and World War II were not a bad time. Air conditioning was then a pasteboard fan with a bird dog on the front and a Levi Garrett ad on the back, and the den was a front porch where old folks sat in rocking chairs and swings and talked of the frontier. And children chasing fireflies and each other could stop awhile to let their overheated systems develop summer colds and hear ancient kinsmen recall struggling for a toehold in North Texas and the Indian Territory.

Gainesville had a past. Her people claimed that Texas' first barbed wire was sold in a local hotel lobby. California Street had been the route of the Forty-Niners, and the town was a Butterfield Overland Mail stage stop. A Confederate statue graced the courthouse square, and the high school was once the palace of a United States Senator. Half a dozen other mansions had been built by cattle barons when Cooke and Grayson counties (Gainesville and Sherman) had more people than Tarrant and Dallas (Fort Worth and Dallas). Frank Buck was born in Gainesville, as were Gene Austin and Charles Paddock. And on the eleventh day of the eleventh month at the eleventh hour of the morning, young folks would climb to the courthouse roof to watch the high school band and the legionnaires march in commemoration of the end of a war.

The town had a history, but clearly Gainesville was only part of a much larger stage. The fencing transaction was the only important historic event to have occurred there, and those who were always out of step with the community questioned that, arguing that barbed wire was first marketed in San Antonio. Otherwise Gainesville's fame depended upon visitors and former residents who had done significant things elsewhere. The gold seekers and the riders of the Overland stage were only passing through. The Civil War was fought hundreds of miles away. Senator Joseph Weldon Bailey's forum was in distant Washington City, and the big cattlemen had grazed their herds farther west and across Red River in the Indian Territory. Frank Buck "brought 'em back alive" from Africa, and Gene Austin wrote "My Blue Heaven" in California, or New York, or some other such place. Charlie Paddock's races, which proved him to be "the world's fastest human," were run elsewhere, and the Armistice Day observance concerned a war in France.

To understand Gainesville one had to know not only how the town developed but also something of those who had originated or sojourned there. Perhaps Cooke County had imparted some special quality which figured in their successes, but certainly the accomplishments of those native sons had had an effect upon Gainesville, where the *Daily Register* recalled with pride their local connections.

The fact that Gainesville was Senator Bailey's town had a shaping effect on the people (Legend was that the mayor and aldermen always met his train and carried him bodily to the old Turner Hotel—"Joe Bailey's feet never touched the ground in Gainesville"), just as the visits of a farmer named Autry to my father's grocery store made an impression on me. His nephew was a Tioga boy who was in the movies. Every Saturday I would inquire after Gene Autry's health, and the old man—who probably had not seen this relative in a decade—always assured me that Gene was faring well, a connection which gave special meaning to his appearances in the Plaza Theater's shoot-em-up, foot-and-onion shows. Any number of us modeled ourselves after Gene Autry; he was a nexus with the world, as were Dwight Eisenhower, of Grayson County, and Chester Nimitz, of Kerr County, and John Nance Garner, of Uvalde County.

By the same reasoning a study of Texas history must include the state's influence upon her absent sons as well as the effect of their deeds upon those who remained here. Taking this broad view, that the state's history comprehends Texans past and present, domestic and foreign—and even honorary—this book reflects brief investigations of a few Texas places and individuals with Texas affiliations whose stories have interested me. Many of these Texans were born elsewhere and spent years building the state, but two, Moses Austin and Dan Inouye, visited for only a few days.

The sketches are in rough chronological order. Hopefully they will add a valuable dimension to traditional Texas history.

Sister Frances Marie Manning gave me her good counsel on grammar and clarity. A number of Texans helped me locate materials, and my secretary, Kathryn Pokladnik, with pure heart and clear head, translated my handwriting into manuscript and endured the entire ordeal.

June Rayfield Welch
University of Dallas
June, 1974

Table of Contents

vii

People and Places
in the Texas Past

by June Rayfield Welch

Indians Painted A Concho County Cliff

For hundreds of years before the white man came to that country Indians sojourned along the Concho River and left pictographs on a sixty-foot bluff northwest of present Paint Rock. Between the cliff and the river, some 300 yards away, lies a plain crossed by a major Indian trail; casual excavation has revealed level upon level of campsites there. For a distance of half a mile the face of the cliff is covered by approximately 1500 paintings, some a thousand years old. That this site was a special place to men who lived or camped there is indicated by the total absence of pictographs on the limestone bluff immediately west of the painted rocks.

Not all of the original paintings have survived; only a fraction still remains. The existing pictographs were executed on rocks previously coated with a beige-colored mineral deposit, the result of seepage from the cliff. Apparently that base permitted the paintings to withstand water and sun. Most are as fresh today as when Forrest Kirkland copied them forty years ago. The limestone which did not have a layer of the mineral could not retain the drawings; flecks of paint on the dull gray stones indicate that they were once decorated, although the designs have vanished.

Four colors were used in the paintings, red, orange, black, and white. Red predominates, perhaps because it suggested blood and life. Black may have symbolized death, as did the upside-down rendition of a man. Many of the drawings were superimposed upon earlier ones. Others have been obliterated by scratching, gouging, or, in some cases, using them as rifle targets. A few of the paintings were destroyed by efforts to chip them loose for removal. Names of white men have been written over some pictographs, the earliest having an 1856 date. Other signatures, more than a century old, are as fresh and clear as if they had been recently executed.

The illustrations are crudely done; the men are usually stick figures; however, one painting appears to be a man in a buffalo headdress. There are representations of birds, snakes, horses, turkeys, wolves or dogs, and buffalo. Handprints abound; for some the artist simply held his paint-covered palm to the rock, and others were made by painting or spraying the hand, leaving only an outline. Many handprints reflect missing fingers or joints. Some of the stick figures hold bows, and one man is shown with a barbed arrow through his head.

A few pictographs definitely date from historic times; those representing horses had to be made after the Spaniards introduced that animal to the new world in the sixteenth century. A fine drawing of a devil, with pointed tail, horns, and pitchfork, was obviously done after the Franciscans came, as was a picture of a church, with towers and crosses.

Many have speculated about the meanings of the various paintings. Most are probably casual markings, doodles. Some were attempts to render the world artistically. A few were messages. Some commemorated important events; the drawing of the church has been thought to represent the burning of the San Sabá mission or the earlier San Clemente mission, both destroyed by Indians. Judge Otto Goetz, asserting that most of the paintings were chronicles of important events, wrote:

> There are more than 1500 of these paintings, or pictographs, some in groups, others by themselves, ranging from the crude to the more symmetrical and artistic. They can be classified as representing commemorations of treaties; meetings of tribes or chieftains; ceremonial performances, as prayers for rain, the replenish-

For perhaps a thousand years men left drawings on this Concho County cliff; some 1,500 remain.

ing of the grasslands; increase of the buffalo herds; the pictographic record of the transition period from the prehistoric to the coming of the Spaniards; the missionaries and the Christian influence; the coming of the God-dog, the horse (strangely pictured at first until the Indians became familiar with them); the strange hogan; the covered wagon drawn by the tamed buffalo (oxen); the long sticks spitting fire from its throat (the white man's gun); the abduction of children, both boys and girls, to be adopted into the tribe; the coming of the longhorn Texas steer; and soldiers, represented by pennants.

To give the pictographs some protection from the weather, Judge Goetz proposed construction of a roof and gutter along the top of the cliff to keep rainwater from draining over them, for he noted that:

> The Painted Rocks of Concho County are a vast storehouse, an archive library of historical information on the lives of the aborigines, written in signs, symbols and figures not yet properly understood. When once correctly interpreted they will supply the missing pages in our continental history.

It was his discovery of the painted rocks that inspired Forrest Kirkland to make his study of Texas pictographs; he began on June 20, 1934, copying the drawings, intent upon preserving the images for later study. Of his first view of the Paint Rock site he wrote:

> A hurried look over the cliff and at the paintings convinced me that no one with whom I had talked had seemed to fully appreciate the significance of these pictographs.... they were badly weathered. Some had been injured by sightseers and many of them had been totally destroyed by ruthless vandals. Here was a veritable gallery of primitive art at the mercy of the elements and the hand of a destructive people. In a few more years only the hundreds of deeply carved names and smears of modern paint will remain to mark the site of the paintings left by the Indians.

The vandalism hazard was overestimated by Kirkland, the administrators of the D. E. Sims estate having guarded them from damage by humans. However, Kirkland's sense of urgency was fortunate in that it induced him and his wife to devote much of the next eight years to copying Indian art at some 80 Texas locations. They preserved the images of thousands of specimens which might not otherwise remain when scholars finally are able to interpret them.

4

The white man added his initials and names to the Indian record.

This pictograph is perhaps an Indian wearing a buffalo headdress. The object below the horns on the left is thought to represent speech, although my guide claimed the Indian was chewing bubble gum.

The center pictograph appears to be a shield; one writer believed it symbolized the affiliation of several tribes.

Spanish Fort Was A Taovaya Village

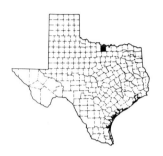

Spanish Fort was inhabited for centuries before the arrival of white men. This may have been due to a good Red River crossing nearby (which was later used by Kansas-bound trail herds), a convenient salt deposit (which served the needs of the inhabitants and attracted game), and terrain which could be easily defended.

Some writers believe the Spanish Fort site was visited by Coronado and the De Soto-Moscoso expedition. The location may have been occupied by the Caddo earlier, but by the middle of the 18th century it was held by the Tawehash Indians. The Tawehash, called Taovaya and Jumano by the Spaniards, were part of the Wichita confederacy. Bénard de la Harpe had encountered them on the Canadian River in present Oklahoma in 1719; the Taovaya had acquired horses and rode them Spanish style, using bridles and saddles. The Comanche and Osage forced them southward in the next few years. Tremiño, a Spanish captive, said the Taovaya settlement at present Spanish Fort was fairly new in 1759.

The Taovaya raised corn, tobacco, pumpkins, beans, melons and sweet potatoes in well-fenced fields. Most of the work was done by women and slaves. The men hunted and fished, although fish apparently served only as fertilizer. Tobacco was traded to the Comanche for horses and buffalo skins. The women wore loose deerskin robes decorated with bear claws. The trousers of the men were held up by buffalo-hide belts ornamented with scalps; they used bows and arrows as well as rifles supplied by the French. They made pots from Red River clay. Animal bones were saved to make tools, weapons, and ornaments; and remnants of their bone piles existed into modern times.

In the late 18th century the Taovaya village consisted of 123 grass huts, each large enough to accomodate ten or twelve beds. The ruler, the Great Bear, was chosen by the populace, including women, on the basis of courage; he owned no property. The Taovaya practiced cannibalism and believed in a life after death. Athanase de Mézières named the village San Teodoro for the commanding general of the Spanish Internal Provinces, Don Teodoro de Croix. The Wichita settlement of 37 grass lodges north of Red River De Mézières called San Bernardo for Governor Bernardo de Galvez. During the American Revolution De Mézières, acting for Spain, made a treaty with the Taovaya; the tomahawk was buried ceremonially, and the Indians gave up two Spanish cannons they had held for two decades.

Spanish traders established themselves at the village, but within a short time many of the Indians died of smallpox. San Teodoro still existed in 1806; the Taovaya, decimated by illness and warfare, finally moved to Oklahoma and became part of the Wichita proper.

The Taovaya village marker faces Spanish Fort's sole operating business, the Coon Hunters Association, whose members live all over the world.

The Taovaya Village Flew A French Flag

The Spaniards, in 1757, established the Mission San Sabá de la Santa Cruz near present Menard for the Apache, which offended the Comanche, Taovaya, and Tonkawa; they attacked the mission on March 16, 1758, massacred the priests, and beseiged the nearby presidio, commanded by Colonel Diego Ortiz Parrilla.

In the following year Parrilla took some 400 ill-trained soldiers and militia and about 250 Indians—including 134 Apache—into North Texas. Going from San Antonio to San Sabá, Parrilla turned northward, crossing the Concho River near the painted rocks. Fifty-five warriors were killed and 149 captives taken at a Tonkawa village in present Shackleford County; the Tonkawa still had horses taken at San Sabá. The captives were later sold as slaves in San Antonio.

Parrilla reached the vicinity of present Spanish Fort on October 7. His scouts encountered a few Indians, who attacked and then retreated. The pursuing Spaniards were amazed when they saw the Taovaya village. It flew the French flag and was well-fortified, "a pueblo formed of high-thatched, oval-shaped houses, surrounded by a stockade and a ditch, the road leading to it being surrounded in the same way . . . with the opening at the very river . . . and all the stockade on that side surmounted by Indians armed with muskets." Anticipating a Spanish attack the Taovaya had dug four cellars for the non-combatants; apparently they were hardly used since the housetops were covered with women and children watching the battle.

The Spaniards had never met such a well-prepared Indian enemy; fire from the stockade was accurate, and the mounted warriors outside the fort were supported by footmen. A Spaniard wrote:

> This heathen captain bore himself . . . with well-ordered valor and dexterity in the management of horse and arms, those which he used being the lance and fusils, which the footmen or servants furnished him. He had a shield of white buckskin and a helmet of the same, with a plume of red horsehair, and he was mounted on a horse of the best qualities and properties . . . .

The Taovaya and their allies, including Comanche, numbered some 6,000 by one estimate. They kept the Spaniards on the defensive, which did not permit effective use of their six cannons. By dark Parrilla had suffered 52 casualties, dead, wounded, and missing, and his men were deserting. Abandoning two cannons, Parrilla retreated to the San Sabá presidio. The failure of Spain at the Taovaya village rankled for years. De Mézières finally recovered the cannons in 1778.

The first Montague County settlers assumed Spaniards had built the old fort. Captain W. A. Norris said walls standing in 1859 showed that there had been six circular fortifications about 150 yards apart in a north-south line surrounded by a stockade and ditch. The walls had port-holes about four feet above the ground.

The Comanche and other Taovaya allies remained outside the fortification and fought Parrilla's army in these fields near Spanish Fort.

William Goyens Was A Freedman

William Goyens was born in North Carolina in 1794; his slave grandfather had been freed because of his Revolutionary War army service. In 1820 Goyens settled at Nacogdoches, which had been nearly obliterated by the Spanish reaction to the Guitérrez-Magee and James Long rebellions. Stephen F. Austin wrote that Nacogdoches had only five houses and a church still standing in 1821.

Goyens was a gunsmith and owned a blacksmith shop. He made wagons, hauled freight between Nacogdoches and Natchitoches, Louisiana, and operated an inn near the present courthouse. Active in civic affairs, he made frequent appearances in the alcalde's court representing other litigants. He owned four slaves when the 1831 census was taken.

Goyens married Mary Sibley, a widowed white woman originally from Georgia, in 1832. She had a son, Henry, by her first marriage, but no children by Goyens. Although Goyens prospered, he was always in danger; freed blacks were a menace to a slave society. Masters feared the presence of freedmen would make their slaves want to escape. Slave catchers attempted to sell freedmen into slavery, and the victims could expect little support from their neighbors.

When Bele Yngles claimed to own him, Goyens got Yngles to agree to accept 1,000 pesos for his claim. Goyens then bought a slave woman from one Llorea for 500 pesos, and Yngles accepted her in return for a complete release. Unfortunately, Goyens had given Llorea a note for the purchase price of the woman; Llorea then claimed he owned Goyens. The alcalde intervened in Goyen's behalf. Other attempts were made, but Goyens remained free, usually by paying a ransom. He was also able to resist attempts to force him, as a freedman, to leave Texas. Inadequate law enforcement contributed to his vulnerability. In 1828, General Manuel Mier y Teran wrote of Nacogdoches, "There are neither civil authorities nor magistrates; one insignificant little man . . . who is called an alcalde, and an ayuntamiento that does not convene once in a lifetime, is the most that we have here at this important point on our frontier . . . ."

Goyens represented the Mexicans in negotiations with the Indians and later served the Texans in the same capacity. In 1835 General T. J. Rusk wrote Cherokee chieftains Bowles and Big Mush:

> Your talks have reached us by the hand of your friend William Goings
> . . . We have heard that you wish Mr. Goings to go with you and hear the talk.
> We are willing that he should go because we believe him to be a man that
> will not tell a lie either for the White man or the Red man.

After the revolution Goyens farmed and operated a grist mill and a lumber mill west of Nacogdoches on the Camino Real. Goyens died June 20, 1857, owning five slaves and 12,423 acres of land in Nacogdoches, Angelina, and Houston counties. His executor valued the land at $7,920; Diane Prince, in her fine thesis, noted that a Nacogdoches realtor had appraised Goyens' land at $1,863,450 in 1967.

William Goyens evaded slave catchers to remain a substantial Nacogdoches businessman. The stone marker is discolored on the sides where cattle rub against it.

Josiah Wilbarger Was Scalped And Lived

Josiah Wilbarger was born in Kentucky and lived in Missouri before moving to Texas in 1827. He settled near present Bastrop, as did his brother, Mathias; Wilbarger County was named for them. Another brother, John Wesley, reached Texas in 1837 and published his *Indian Depredations in Texas* fifty years later.

Josiah's farm, seventy-five miles from the nearest residence, made him the "outside settler" until Reuben Hornsby settled below present Austin in 1832. There were always visitors at the homes of outside settlers, travelers heading west and those planning to settle in the neighborhood. They brought news and afforded assistance in case of Indian troubles.

Wilbarger, a surveyor, was always interested in new country. In August, 1833, he stopped at Hornsby's place. Several others were there at the time. With four companions Wilbarger set out into the new land. Northwest of Austin they pursued, without result, an Indian. At noon they camped four miles east of the Austin site and were eating lunch when Indians attacked, shooting Christian and Strother. Wilbarger had a hip wound and arrows in both legs. His horse was unsaddled and hobbled, and as he ran to catch a ride with Standifer an Indian shot him; the bullet passed through his neck. Haynie and Standifer escaped. Although Wilbarger appeared to be dead he was conscious as the Indians took his clothes, scalped him, and cut the throats of Christian and Strother.

That afternoon Wilbarger crawled into a pool; he drank and lay there until he began to chill. He tried to reach Hornsby's but was exhausted after covering a fraction of the six miles. He spent the night beneath an oak tree, naked, numb from the cold, and with maggots invading his wounds. As he slept he dreamed of his sister, Margaret Clifton; he would learn later that she died the day before in Missouri. Mrs. Clifton told him to remain beneath the tree and he would be rescued. Then she departed toward Hornsby's.

At Hornsby's, Haynie and Standifer had reported the three deaths and that they saw an Indian take Wilbarger's hair. But Mrs. Hornsby had a dream that night, too. She roused Hornsby and the others, insisting that she had seen Wilbarger beneath a tree, naked and scalped, but alive. Early the next morning they went searching for Wilbarger. When they saw him, Wilbarger appeared to be an Indian because of sunburn and the dried blood covering his body. Sensing their mistake he called, "Don't shoot, it is Wilbarger." The only clothing the Indians had left him was a sock, which he was wearing on his head to protect the wound.

Wilbarger lived eleven years. The scalp loss permitted his skull to become diseased, and he died from accidentally bumping his head on a door frame. His son, John, was killed in 1850 as he and two other rangers were attacked by Indians; Wilbarger and Sullivan died; their wounded companion escaped. John Wilbarger was buried beside his father at Bastrop, but later Josiah was moved to the State Cemetery.

This Bastrop house, built in 1842, has been occupied by Josiah Wilbarger's descendants for a century and a quarter.

José Ruíz Signed the Declaration of Texas Independence

Spanish-born tailor Juan Manuel Ruíz settled in San Antonio about 1760 and married Manuela de la Pena of Saltillo, Mexico. Their son, José, and grandson, José Antonio Navarro, were the only native Texans to sign the Declaration of Independence. Juan Ruíz died in 1797 at the age of sixty.

José Francisco Ruíz, was born in San Antonio, September 1, 1780. Educated in Spain, he became San Antonio's first school teacher in 1803; his home, south of the Military Plaza, was the first public school. He married Josepha Hernandez and helped manage his father's ranch. Ruíz, an early advocate of Mexican independence, supported the Morelos revolution and had to flee after the insurgents were defeated. Living in the United States from 1813 to 1822, he returned to San Antonio after Mexico became independent of Spain.

After his return Ruíz managed his ranches and took part in public affairs. When Bustamante issued the Law of April 6, 1830, designed to restrict American colonization, Ruíz objected. He had assisted Austin's colonists, particularly with Indian problems. As a colonel of the San Antonio garrison, Ruíz was ordered to build a fort at the Camino Real crossing of the Brazos River for use in enforcing the restrictions on immigration. He established Fort Tenoxtitlan near present Bryan in July, 1830; his command numbered some 70 soldiers.

In spite of his position Ruíz remained a friend of the colonists and supported Bustamante's opponent, Santa Anna, who became president of Mexico in 1832. The Texans, who thought Santa Anna would grant their requests, including statehood separate from Coahuila, were alarmed when Santa Anna followed his predecessor's course. In May, 1835, Santa Anna set aside the Constitution of 1824 and became dictator. Mexican troops were sent into Texas, and the first fighting occurred at Gonzales on October 2, as the Mexicans tried to seize a cannon. A consultation of the settlers was held the next month at Washington-on-the-Brazos, and a provisional government was formed as Santa Anna assembled his armies to invade Texas.

The Texans captured San Antonio from General Cós in December, 1835. When a convention was announced for Washington-on-the-Brazos, José Ruíz was elected to represent San Antonio. He signed the Declaration of Texas Independence on March 2, 1836. Although he spoke no English, Ruíz represented San Antonio in the Republic's first Senate. He died in 1840. The San Fernando Cathedral burial record reads:

> In this city of San Fernando de Bexar on the 20th day of January, I, the priest, Don Refugio de la Garza, curate proper of this city, buried in this parish, at a depth of ten feet, the body of Lt. Colonel Don Francisco Ruíz, widower. He made his last will and did not bequeath anything to works of Mercy. He received the Holy Sacrament and died of hydropsy at sixty-one years of age.

This portrait of José Ruíz was in progress at the time of his death. The body was propped up so the artist might finish the work.

17

McKinney Was the Oldest Signer of the Texas Declaration

Collin McKinney, born April 17, 1766, in New Jersey—a subject of George III—died September 8, 1861, in Confederate Texas. He lived through two revolutions and was subject to at least seven sovereigns: England, the American colonies, the United States, Mexico, the Texas provisional government, the Republic of Texas, and the Confederate States of America. He was the oldest signer of the Declaration of Texas Independence.

McKinney married Amy Moore in Lincoln County, Kentucky, in 1792. Two of their four children, Ashley and Polly, lived to maturity. Amy McKinney died in 1804, and McKinney then married Betsy Coleman. Their children were William C., Amy, Peggy, Anna, Eliza, and Younger Scott McKinney.

After Senator George Campbell became the American minister to Russia, McKinney managed Campbell's Tennessee properties. He operated a trading post before moving to Arkansas, six miles east of present Texarkana, on September 15, 1824. In 1831 he settled in present Bowie County.

McKinney was chosen to represent the Red River country in the 1835 consultation, and he was elected to the convention at Washington-on-the-Brazos the next March. As Santa Anna beseiged the Alamo, the delegates met; McKinney was appointed to a five-man committee which was to present an instrument declaring Texas independence. On the following day, March 2, 1836, the draft, probably brought to Texas by George Childress, was adopted by the delegates. The presiding officer, Judge Richard Ellis, wrote, "There was something about Mr. McKinney's personality that drew the delegates to him . . . .He was slow to reach conclusions, but when he made up his mind he could not be easily made to change." Another delegate said:

> But one time during the convention did he exhibit impatience. That was when Mr. Everett proposed a postponement of action on the committee report submitting the Declaration of Independence. When this was done, Mr. McKinney arose from his seat and made a brief but impassionate speech against delaying action. When he sat down Mr. Everett withdrew his resolution.

McKinney was a member of the First, Second, and Fourth Congresses of the Republic. He advocated making counties as nearly thirty miles square as possible, with the courthouse near the geographic center, so that citizens could vote without undue hardship. This was important when travel was by horse or "footback and walking."

In 1884 he moved into present Collin County. When the first state legislature carved several counties from Fannin, one was named Collin. Buckner, the first capitol, was not centrally located, so McKinney, laid out in 1848, became the county seat.

After he was 75 years old, McKinney made eleven trips guiding Kentuckians and Tennesseans to new homes in North Texas, where he helped establish the Disciples of Christ.

The Collin McKinney home was moved from its original location north of McKinney.

Francisco Ruíz Was Ordered To Bury the Alamo Defenders

Francisco Antonio Ruíz, the 31-year-old son of José Francisco Ruíz, was the alcalde of San Antonio when Santa Anna put the Alamo under siege. His father and cousin, José Navarro, were at Washington-on-the Brazos, where they signed the Declaration of Texas Independence on March 2, 1836. Aware of the sympathies of the Ruíz family, Santa Anna lodged two officers in the alcalde's home to keep an eye on him.

On Sunday morning, March 6, Santa Anna ordered Ruíz to come to the river. Ruíz wrote:

Santa Anna directed me to call on some of the neighbors to come with carts to carry the (Mexican) dead to the cemetery and to accompany him as he was desirous to have colonels Travis, Bowie, and Crockett shown to him. On the north battery of the fortress convent lay the lifeless body of Colonel Travis on the gun carriage shot only through the forehead. Towards the west and in a small fort opposite the city we found the body of Colonel Crockett. Colonel Bowie was found dead in his bed in one of the rooms on the south side.

Santa Anna, after all the Mexican bodies had been taken out, ordered wood to be brought to burn the bodies of the Texans. He sent a company of dragoons with me to bring wood and dry branches from the neighboring forests. About three o'clock in the afternoon of March 6th we laid the wood and dry branches upon which a pile of dead bodies were placed, more wood was piled on them and another pile of dead bodies was brought, and in this manner they were all arranged in layers. Kindling wood was distributed through the pile and about five o'clock in the evening it was lighted.

The dead Mexicans of Santa Anna were taken to the graveyard, but not having sufficient room for them I ordered some to be thrown into the river, which was done on the same day.

The gallantry of the few Texans who defended the Alamo was really wondered at by the Mexican Army. Even the generals were astonished at their vigorous resistance and how dearly victory was bought.

The generals who under Santa Anna participated in the storming of the Alamo were Juan Amador, Castrillion, Ramirez, Sesma, and Andrade.

The men burnt (Alamo defenders) were one hundred and eighty-two. I was an eyewitness for as alcalde of San Antonio I was, with some of the neighbors, collecting the dead bodies and placing them on the funeral pyre.

Ruíz served as a San Antonio alderman from 1837 to 1841. Opposed to the annexation of Texas, he believed that those who arrived after 1836 should have no voice in deciding whether Texas should remain independent. When statehood came Ruíz, exasperated, moved beyond the frontier and lived with the Indians. In his last years he returned to San Antonio, where he died October 18, 1876, in the house which had belonged to his grandfather and father. The house, almost 200 years old, was damaged by a hurricane in 1942. It was moved to the Witte Museum the next year.

The 200-year-old Ruíz house accomodated San Antonio's first public school. Damaged by a hurricane in 1942, it was moved from Military Plaza to the Witte Museum.

Johanna Troutman Designed a Texas Flag

When the Texas revolution began, eighteen-year-old Johanna Troutman helped recruit the Georgia Battalion. With Colonel William Ward in command, three companies of 112 Georgians reached Texas in December, 1835, bringing with them a flag designed by Johanna Troutman. The white silk flag bore a five-pointed blue star and the legend "Liberty or Death."

The Lone Star Flag was first flown at Velasco on January 8, 1836. At Goliad, Colonel James W. Fannin had it raised as the ensign of the Republic of Texas after hearing that the delegates at Washington-on-the-Brazos had adopted the Declaration of Texas Independence. The flag was destroyed in the fighting at Goliad. The Georgia Battalion, which by then included a fourth company, the Mobile Grays, was at Refugio when captured by Mexican troops and returned to Goliad. There most of the battalion and its commanding officer, Colonel Ward, died in the Goliad Massacre.

Johanna Troutman Pope died in Alabama in 1880. Governor Oscar B. Colquitt arranged for her reburial in the State Cemetery at Austin in 1913.

The body of Joanna Troutman was moved from Alabama to the State Cemetery at Austin.

Gail Borden Laid Out the City of Houston

Gail Borden, Jr., came to Texas in 1829 after his brother, Tom, had written about opportunities in the Austin Colony. After the Law of April 6, 1830, forbade immigration from the United States, Gail Borden was a member of the San Felipe Committee of Correspondence. He was also a delegate to the Convention of 1833.

Soon after the revolution began, Borden and two partners began publication of *The Telegraph and Texas Register* at San Felipe. Although nine other papers had been established, none lasted more than two years. To avoid Santa Anna's troops, Borden moved the paper to Harrisburg and then Columbia. During the revolution *The Telegraph* was, in the words of Dr. Joe B. Frantz, "the voice of Texas." After the Allen brothers announced plans for a new town—Houston—Gail and Tom Borden were hired to survey and plat the Buffalo Bayou site. In May, 1837, *The Telegraph* became Houston's first newspaper; shortly thereafter Gail Borden sold his interest and became the Galveston customs collector.

Galveston Island then was barely inhabited; however, it grew from two families in 1837 to 1,500 residents two years later when Borden became the agent of the Galveston City Company. In twelve years he sold 2,500 lots and the population reached 4,200, making Galveston the state's largest city.

Borden began inventing at Galveston. His locomotive bathhouse provided dressing rooms for men and women on opposite sides and partitioned off what otherwise would have been mixed bathing; it could be dragged out of the water when not in use. Borden's yard was littered with the wreckage of ill-conceived inventions, and Galvestonians considered him eccentric. Always believing the next project would succeed, he kept on, in the process developing a philosophy upon which he would found an industrial giant: the way of the future lay in making objects smaller. He developed the meat bisquit, made of dried beef and flour. For the meat bisquit Borden received one of the five gold medals presented American inventors at the 1851 Great Council Exhibition held in Queen Victoria's London. Borden's dream of pioneers and armies subsisting on compact, non-spoiling, meat bisquit was not to be realized. It had a bad taste and caused nausea.

Borden impoverished himself and his friends in the meat bisquit effort, and he moved to New York seeking capital. As his meat bisquit hopes dimmed, he began trying to condense milk. His 1853 patent application for condensing milk in a vacuum was granted in 1856. The early attempts at manufacturing failed, but with Jeremiah Milbank's help the third company succeeded. During the Civil War, the New York Condensed Milk Company flourished; it was the genesis of the Borden Company, which was, in 1972, a dairy, food, and chemical concern with sales of $2.2 billion and 47,000 employees, 200 factories, and 7,500 products.

Borden died January 11, 1874, at Borden, Texas, and was buried in White Plains, New York, in a plot that had been marked by a huge granite milk can.

Gail Borden laid out the city of Houston, published Houston's first newspaper, and founded the Borden Company.

Johnston Dueled for Command of the Texas Army

Kentuckian Albert Sidney Johnston graduated from West Point in 1826; from the beginning he was regarded as a brilliant young officer. In 1834 Johnston resigned his commission and began farming in order to care for his seriously ill wife. After her death, and not certain what he wanted to do, he met Stephen F. Austin, who was in Louisville seeking help for the Texans.

Johnston reached Nacogdoches in July, 1836. The war had ended suddenly. Sam Houston was in New Orleans for medical treatment, and T. J. Rusk had command of the unruly Texas Army; it was agitated by volunteers who had come too late for battle and wanted to lynch the captive Santa Anna. Johnston joined the army as a private, but Rusk promoted him to colonel and then made him adjutant general. The malcontents had elected Felix Huston major general; Rusk warned Johnston about Huston. While Johnston was in New Orleans on business, President Houston made him the senior brigadier general and in January, 1837, gave Johnston command of the army. In the meantime Huston had taken charge. A Kentuckian and natural leader, Huston was ambitious and overbearing, without military experience but intent upon building a reputation and subsequent political career. Huston announced that he would resist any attempt to displace him; his success as a duelist made his meaning clear.

When Johnston returned to camp Huston sent a note stating:

> You, in assuming the command under an appointment connected with the attempt to ruin my reputation . . . of course stand in an attitude of opposition to myself . . . I therefore propose a meeting between us.

Johnston accepted the challenge. There being no dueling pistols available they would use Huston's horse pistols, which Jefferson Davis described as "crook-handled, twelve inches in the barrel." Johnston's acceptance of the pistols was surprising, since he would have had the advantage with rapiers. Another disadvantage was the requirement that they shoot from the hip.

Johnston, aware of his plight, had to keep Huston from taking aim. His son wrote:

> It is known to those familiar with the use of the hair-trigger that if the finger is allowed to touch it the report of another pistol will almost always produce a sufficient involuntary muscular contraction of the finger to cause a premature discharge. Availing himself of this fact, General Johnston raised his pistol quickly, and, with his eye on his opponent's finger, just anticipated him enough to succeed in drawing his fire before he could cover him with his pistol. He repeated this five times with the same result, much to Huston's discomfiture, whose reputation as a "dead shot" was at stake . . . At the sixth shot Huston's superior skill prevailed, and General Johnston fell, with a ball through his hip.

Johnston remained near death for weeks. Huston's victory was popular at first, but then sentiment began to change and Huston left the army. Johnston was able to return to duty in December, 1837, and a few months later he became Lamar's Secretary of War.

Elisabet Ney executed this bust of Albert Sidney Johnston as well as the recumbent statue at his tomb in the State Cemetery.

Bigfoot Wallace Was the Texas Dan Boone

William Alexander Anderson Wallace, born in Lexington, Virginia, April 3, 1817, had hoped to avenge the death of his brother, Samuel, at Goliad, but the San Jacinto victory made that impossible. Arriving at Galveston in October, 1837, he went to Bastrop, then to La Grange. He met Sam Houston while applying for his brother's revolutionary war land grant. Wallace killed his first Indian after a war party took most of the horses in the neighborhood.

In April, 1838, he moved to San Antonio, where the Alamo ruins had not been touched since Santa Anna's seige and some of the defenders' bones remained in the ashes of the funeral pyre. After Austin became the capital, Wallace went there. An expert with the broad-axe, he hired out to hew logs for the government buildings at $200 a month. The high pay was due to the Indian hazard; war parties had killed forty Austin residents.

Wallace soon found hunting and selling the meat in Austin more to his taste than swinging an axe. Once he chased a small buffalo herd down Congress Avenue, which was marked only by surveyor's stakes; the buffalo swam the Colorado River at the foot of the street. His most lasting contribution was digging, for a saloon keeper, Austin's first well.

Wallace and William Fox hauled building stone from the hills; it was Fox who gave Wallace his nickname. A huge Waco Indian, whose moccasin tracks measured fourteen inches, had been killing and stealing in Austin. When the bigfooted Indian robbed a settler and his tracks led to the Fox and Wallace cabin, the settler accused Wallace, who wore moccasins, stood six feet two inches, and weighed 240 pounds. After Wallace put his much shorter foot in the big track the settler apologized, but Fox always called Wallace "Bigfoot" after that. Later Fox was killed and scalped by the big Waco, who was trailed by Wallace many times, without success.

Wallace was among the first members of John Hays' ranger company. At San Antonio they dispatched a number of badmen, and in 1842 Wallace took part in the fighting after Mexican General Adrian Woll invaded San Antonio. Wallace was one of the fortunate members of the Mier Expedition who drew white beans after the Hacienda Salado escape; Santa Anna had ordered the execution of seventeen men, whose fate was determined by drawing black beans from a pitcher.

As the country filled up, Wallace moved to the Medina River below Castroville, where he explored and did ranger duty. After service in the Mexican War, in 1850 Wallace began carrying the mail between San Antonio and El Paso, a month-long, 600-mile journey through Comanche country. Moving again he settled on Chacon Creek, five miles from present Devine. He captained a ranger company whose 76 men included Edward Westfall, the killer of the bigfooted Waco. Later Wallace captured runaway slaves. He was in Virginia when John Brown raided Harper's Ferry, but he opposed the secession of Texas.

In his last years Wallace was badly palsied, but his eyes were good and he had all his teeth, although they were worn off to the gums. He died January 7, 1899.

Bigfoot Wallace kept moving westward as civilization approached.

The Ship Channel Made Houston a Major City

Houston was founded upon water transport, a rare asset in early Texas. After Santa Anna's army destroyed Harrisburg it was possible to found a new town on Buffalo Bayou, which was deep enough for freighting and, unlike the Brazos, remained so in all seasons. August C. and John K. Allen bought land eight miles above Harrisburg at the navigable point farthest inland. Hoping it would become the new capital, the Allens named the town for President Houston. After the penniless new government was given free building lots, Houston was made the capital on November 30, 1836.

Governor Francis R. Lubbock wrote of a January, 1837, boat trip to Houston, which took three days because of obstacles in the channel:

> Just before reaching our destination a party of us, becoming weary of the steamer, took a yawl and concluded we would hunt for the city. So little evidence did we see of a landing that we passed by the site.

Houston was a tent city, but Sam Houston estimated the population at 1,500 in April. When Austin became the capital, in 1839, Houston was damaged, but it remained a trading center. Freight was still moved down the bayou in shallow-draft vessels and loaded on ships at Galveston. Cotton, lumber, and livestock from the interior were sold at Houston, where farmers could buy supplies they could not raise or make.

Buffalo Bayou was easily navigable to Harrisburg but the Houston channel was narrow, filled with snags and obstructions, and overhung with tree limbs. The first effort to improve the channel facilitated navigation but did not solve the problems; two steamboats sank after striking snags. The Port of Houston was established in 1841, and the Republic made grants to clear obstructions. The coming of the railroads increased freight volume at Houston, and the Galveston Wharf Company's high rates caused ship owners to seek an alternative harbor. Except for Jefferson's inland traffic, Galveston had a virtual monopoly on water freight. Howard Peak wrote:

> At this time Galveston was the only real city in Texas. Its strategic location, her command of the import and export business, and her great aggregation of capital conspired to make it the first city of the state.

Work on a nine-foot channel from Houston to the Gulf began in 1870. With Houston designated a port of entry, federal funds became available, and the Morgan Steamship Company, the largest shipping firm in the Gulf, cut a canal which permitted vessels to avoid Clopper's Bar, a sandbar at the confluence of the Bayou and the San Jacinto River. The Morgan company bought the Bayou channel company and, with federal help, dredged a twelve-foot channel to its new town, Clinton, below Harrisburg. Clinton was linked by rail with Houston, eight miles away. In September, 1876, the first ocean-going vessel, came up the channel. The *New Orleans Times* said, "At Clinton all future freight and passengers will be transferred for all interior points in Texas instead of Galveston, as formerly."

By 1908 the channel was 18½ feet deep and a turning basin had been completed. In 1929 Houston was the nation's eighth ranking port and now ranks third in seaport tonnage.

Houston's ship channel borders the San Jacinto battleground, where the battleship *Texas* is permanently moored.

John B. Denton Was Killed at Village Creek

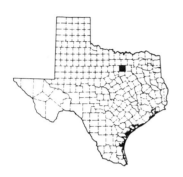

There were few settlers in north Texas in 1838. Fannin County was on the frontier. In present Tarrant County several hundred Indians, Cherokee, Shawnee, Delaware, Kickapoo, Choctaw, Alabama, Coushatta, and Caddo, had established themselves on Village Creek in present Tarrant County. Incited by Vicente Cordova, a Mexican agent, the Indians raided the northeast, which lost half its population. As a result punitive expeditions were made to the upper Trinity, an area thought to be wasteland. General Hugh McLeod reflected the surprise of the volunteers, writing that it was "the finest portion of Texas as a body, and its bottoms are equally as fine as the Brazos. We saw large droves of buffalo and wild horses, by the latter I do not mean mustangs such as are found in western Texas — the Ukraine cannot excel these prairies in the beauty, and fleetness of its wild horses."

The Texas Congress authorized the formation of militia companies for frontier protection in February, 1841. After Indians attacked the John Yeary home in Fannin County and massacred the Ripley family in present Titus County, volunteers began assembling at Choctaw Bayou, in present Grayson County, to drive the Indians from the upper Trinity. James Bourland was elected captain of the seventy men and William C. Young, lieutenant. Militia Brigadier General Edward H. Tarrant joined as a member, but assumed command during the campaign.

On May 14, 1841, the volunteers departed; not knowing the base of the Indians, they went first to the West Fork of the Trinity near modern Bridgeport, where they destroyed two abandoned villages. They dropped down to the Brazos, found nothing, and returned to the Trinity near present Fort Worth. There an Indian told them of villages located on a creek to the east.

On the morning of May 24, the men charged the first town, General Tarrant saying, "Now, my brave men, we will never all meet on earth again." It was taken, and as survivors were pursued along the creek a second village was reached and captured. The militiamen then found a third town which extended for a mile and a half along the creek. They encountered substantial resistance but were successful. Tarrant mustered the company and found that all of his men were alive. There were 225 lodges in the three villages; a thousand warriors lived there, but more than half were away hunting.

When John B. Denton took a scouting party into the woods he saw another village. Denton was thirty-four, a Methodist minister born in Tennessee and raised in Indiana. His wife had taught him to read and write. He had lived in Arkansas before coming to Clarksville, where he practiced law; he had preached the first sermon in Fannin County. As Denton was crossing the creek, Indians concealed in the timber loosed a salvo, killing him and wounding Henry Stout. The others retreated. Denton was buried the next morning in present Denton County, some 25 miles from the Indian villages. Later he was reburied on the courthouse square in Denton.

This campaign and a later one caused the Indians to move farther west, opening the Dallas-Fort Worth area to settlement.

Along Tarrant County's Village Creek, near present Handley, lived several hundred Indians who raided northeast Texas settlements.

Houston Signed a Treaty at Bird's Fort

The northern frontier during Sam Houston's first administration, "bled at every pore with Indian depredations and treachery." The westernmost settlement, Holland Coffee's trading post in present Grayson County, had a dozen residents. A few hardy souls were scattered over Fannin and Red River counties, but Clarksville was the only real town. Indian attacks increased after Lamar became president, most of the raiders coming from present Tarrant County.

In 1840 Captain Jonathan Bird, of Bowie County, took forty rangers to the upper Trinity and built near present Euless a palisaded log structure and some houses. General Tarrant had ordered a settlement established, but Bird and his men, unable to get titles to the land, went home. The first white habitation in Tarrant County, occasionally travelers used the Bird's Fort buildings. In late 1841 Mabel Gilbert moved into one of them, but after a few months he decided to join John Neely Bryan; Gilbert took his family down the Trinity's West Fork in two cottonwood canoes; Mrs. Gilbert was the first white woman in Dallas County.

Houston began his second term in December, 1841, intending to solve the Indian problem by substituting trade for warfare; mercantile posts would be established along a boundary separating white and Indians. He wrote, "I do not doubt that this system, once established, would conciliate the Indians, open a lucrative commerce with them, and bring continued peace to our entire frontier." Traders would be protected by about twenty-five men stationed at each post, which would be far less expensive than Lamar's wars.

Houston invited the tribes to a peace council in 1842, but heavy rains kept them away; another was then called for August, 1843, at Bird's Fort. In the meantime the tribes were encouraged to visit the trading house the Torrey brothers were to establish on the Brazos. In late July, with his guide, John Reagan, Houston headed north. A number of tribes were present when Houston arrived, and more came in, but not the Comanche or Wichita. After waiting almost a month, Houston opened the council. To impress the Indians he wore a purple velvet suit embroidered with the heads of foxes and silver spurs. He had a bowie knife at his belt and an Indian blanket thrown over his shoulders. The journey was hard on Houston; he wrote, "Since I started to the Indian Council I have suffered more from my wound (sustained at the battle of Horseshoe Bend) than I have done for the past twenty years."

The Bird's Fort treaty was signed September 29, 1843, by Texas commissioners and representatives of the Delaware, Chickasaw, Waco, Tawakoni, Kichai, Caddo, Anadarko, Ioni, Biloxi and Cherokee. It provided that whites could go west of the boundary only by permission of the president; Indians were not to cross except with consent of an agent. Blacksmiths and teachers were to be sent to the tribes. Congress ratified the treaty in January; most of the Indians retired west of a line extending roughly from Fort Worth to Menard and San Antonio, opening a huge area to peaceful settlement. Fort Worth's first traders departed because of Indian trouble. The second trading house, below modern Arlington, opened in September, 1845.

President Sam Houston journeyed to Bird's Fort to implement a new policy of trading with the Indians instead of fighting them.

Jefferson Was a Port City

Jefferson was laid out in 1842 because of access to New Orleans by way of the Big Cypress and Red rivers. With cheap water transport available, farmers began planting cotton, which had not been profitable because of the cost of hauling by ox wagon. The first steamboat reached Jefferson in 1844; warehouses and docks were built, and businesses opened to accomodate the developing commerce. Jefferson became the Cass County seat in 1845 and incorporated in 1848, rivaling Shreveport as water freight opened huge areas to commercial farming. Jefferson had nearly a thousand citizens in 1860 when it became the capital of the new Marion County; the Cass County government had been moved to Linden.

By 1861 Marion County had four thousand inhabitants, half of them slaves. The taxable value of slaves exceeded that of all other property, including 134,485 acres of land, 872 horses, 2,565 cattle and 194 sheep. Secession sentiment was strong because of the threatened loss of a million dollars worth of slaves. More than a fourth of the whites served in the Confederate Army, and great quanitites of supplies were shipped from Jefferson.

Although reconstruction was difficult, Jefferson reached its peak in those years. Its huge trade territory, extending from Arkansas to Fort Worth, made it the largest city in north Texas. A newspaper reported:

> Jefferson presents a picture of unexampled energy and prosperity. Her mammoth business houses overflowing with merchandise; her levees crowded with steamboats discharging freight that supplies thousands of square miles of interior. Her unbounded resources as a commercial center are illustrated when we take into consideration that the past week nearly 5,000 bales of cotton have been shipped . . .

Estimates of those in Jefferson ranged up to 30,000 because of men present on business and settlers stopping over on their way west. Jefferson's population was 4,190 in 1870, compared to 13,818 for Galveston, Houston's 9,382, and Dallas' 3,000 residents.

One-fourth of Texas' commerce passed through Jefferson. Its navigable channel resulted from the Red River rafts, massive accumulations of debris which backed water into adjoining lakes and bayous. As the water level rose in the winter and early spring, steamers carried freight down Big Cypress River, across Caddo and Soda lakes to Red River and Shreveport or on to the Mississippi and New Orleans. Cotton, wheat, lumber, wool, and hides were stored in Jefferson warehouses pending the rainy season.

As railroads penetrated the interior farmers were no longer so dependent upon Jefferson's port. The removal of the rafts from Red River, completed by 1873, lowered the water level in the Big Cypress, making smaller boats necessary. Jefferson businessmen had long hoped for railroads into the interior to bring freight to their port, but by the time the Texas and Pacific began laying track in 1873 the falling water level had forecast the end of steamship service. Jefferson's population fell to 2,850 according to the 1900 census — only 16 fewer than the number of residents in 1970.

36

Jefferson became the great city of the Texas interior by virtue of the then navigable
Big Cypress.

The Dalby Springs Congregation Has Met Since 1839

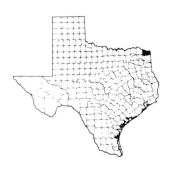

Probably the first Methodist service held in Texas was conducted by William Stevenson in 1815 at the home of Claibourne Wright. The Roman Catholic Church was the established religion of Mexico, but the Pecan-Point-Jonesboro neighborhood of present Red River County was assumed to be in Arkansas. The Sunday School class begun by a Mr. Tidwell at Jonesboro was the first Methodist organization in Texas.

In 1834 the Mississippi Methodist conference sent Henry Stephenson to do missionary work in Texas, although holding Protestant services violated Mexican law. The Methodists were growing rapidly in the United States; their ministers were badly educated but zealous, and as they anticipated the 1839 centennial of Methodism their evangelism was so successful that the 1840 census of the United States would reveal the Methodists to be the most numerous of the denominations.

After William Barret Travis, a few months before his death, wrote to Methodists in the United States asking for ministers to be sent to Texas, Martin Ruter and others responded. Ruter organized some twenty missions within a short time and, appearing before the Congress of the Republic, he urged the establishment of Bastrop University. After his death, in 1838, the institution was founded and named Rutersville College.

Itinerant Methodist ministers preached throughout Texas. One of the oldest active congregations is that at Dalby Springs, Bowie County. Formed in 1839, services of the Dalby Springs Methodist Church were held in homes and beneath the trees until the Civil War period, when a school was begun. The congregation used the schoolhouse until 1887; Jack Whitecotton donated the land upon which the present frame church was constructed.

Dalby Springs was a nineteenth century health resort because of the curative properties of its water. The 1970 census reflected a population of only 65 residents, but people still come to the old Dalby Springs churchyard to fill jugs from the ancient pump.

The Dalby Springs Methodists have used this frame building since 1887.

The Round Rock Marked a Fording Place

Long before the white men came Indians knew that the round rock in Brushy Creek marked a good crossing. When the Ramón-St. Denis expedition of 1716 crossed Williamson County its chronicler referred to Brushy as "The Creek of the Blessed Souls." Later travelers camped near the round rock and forded the stream there because the stone creek bed provided safe passage; it was a natural townsite.

Ferdinand Roemer met a farmer in 1846 who had lived near the round rock for a decade, but settlement actually began about 1843 when Washington Anderson built a gristmill. Jacob Harrell moved there from Austin in 1848. The village was called Brushy Creek when the post office was opened in Thomas Oatts' store in 1852, but after postal officials objected because another Texas town was using that name the community became Round Rock. Mail service provided by private contractors operated from San Antonio through Austin, Round Rock, Georgetown, Waco and Dallas to Memphis, Tennessee. There were only a few slaves in Williamson County, but as the slavery controversy grew the county commissioners appointed a patrol for Georgetown in 1853 and added another at Round Rock three years later.

Old Round Rock was north of Brushy Creek, but after the railroad passed on the south side another town, New Round Rock, grew up; for fifteen years each had a post office. The arrival of the International and Great Northern in 1876 caused a number of Georgetown merchants to move to Round Rock, which, as the terminus of the line, attracted ox wagons serving points as far away as San Antonio.

Prosperity generated by the traffic brought others to Round Rock also. Sam Bass came to hold up a bank. Earlier John Wesley Hardin had lived in Round Rock and attended Greenwood Masonic Institute, but the exploits which made him the worst of the gunmen—killing some thirty men, each of whom, he contended, deserved shooting—occurred elsewhere. Sam Bass had achieved his notoriety in other places, too. Before he was able to carry out his mission in Round Rock he was mortally wounded by a Texas Ranger. Bass died two days later, July 21, 1878—his twenty-seventh birthday—at the Round Rock Hotel.

Clara Stearns Scarbrough, in her superb county history, noted that the hotel proprietor sent the state a bill for the cot, sheet, and pillow he furnished the wounded Bass and that there was speculation in the *Williamson County Sun* concerning the payment of rewards:

> . . . a question arises as to who is entitled to the various rewards offered by the state and railroad companies for the capture of Sam Bass. The Austin *Gazette* is doubtful if any reward can be claimed. The offers, it says, were for the "arrest and conviction." The point raised by the *Gazette* draws it rather too fine. What the state wanted, and what the railroads wanted, was that Sam bas [sic] should be stopped from levying tribute upon railroads and banks. That such operations were stopped by the man who killed him, hardly admits of controversy.

The Round Rock in Brushy Creek marked a safe crossing.

Baylor Opened at Independence

In October, 1840, three Baptist churches—at Travis, Independence, and La Grange—with a total of 45 members, formed the Union Baptist Association; T. W. Cox, who was pastor of all three congregations, and two other preachers, I. L. Davis and R. E. B. Baylor, were present. At the next annual meeting Judge Baylor, the secretary of the association, urged that a Baptist school be founded; his recommendation resulted in the formation of an educational society. By 1843 there were 13 churches in the association — Baptists in Texas probably numbered no more than 300—and the Baptist Education Society was meeting as a separate body under Judge Baylor's leadership.

Baylor and William Tryon were authorized to apply to the Republic for a university charter in 1845. Since a name had to be chosen before Congress could act, Judge Baylor proposed calling it Tryon University, because Tryon had originally suggested founding a college. Instead Tryon wrote Baylor's name into the charter and insisted that it remain. The Congress chartered Baylor University on February 1, 1845.

Bids were sought for location of the institution, and four towns made offers. Independence prevailed over Shannon's Prairie, Huntsville, and Travis by offering a decrepit two-story frame building and land valued at $7,925. Professor Henry Gillette began preparatory instruction with 24 students on May 18, 1846. Enrollment was seventy by the end of the year. Tuition for reading, writing, and spelling was $8.00 for a five-month term. Courses in arithmetic, geography, and grammar cost another $10.00. Students boarded in town for $8.00 a month, and all classes were held in the frame building; the upstairs could not be used because it had no floor. The building was also used for church services by Methodists, Presbyterians, and Baptists on successive Sundays. Gillette was the only teacher that first year and received slightly more than half his $800 salary.

The Reverend Henry Graves became president of Baylor and collegiate instruction was begun in 1847; however, few students were able to do college-level work because of the lack of schools. Judge Baylor and others solicited support for the institution throughout the south, and Reverend James Huckins was hired, for $1000 a year, to raise funds. He was able to get cash gifts in the older states, but Texans donated cattle, horses, and hides. The few thousand dollars he brought in kept the school open. Away for a year at a time, Huckins rode horseback through the northern, eastern and southern states seeking help for Baylor, which hoped for a $10,000 endowment.

The Law Department opened in 1849, with Judge Baylor teaching some courses. Baylor, a Kentuckian, had served in the War of 1812, studied law, and had been a legislator in Kentucky and Alabama before his election to Congress in 1828. A Baptist minister, he was also a district judge and associate justice of the Republic's Supreme Court.

Gillette resigned in 1848, noting that he had taught young Texans for eight years and it was time for others to undertake that ordeal. By 1850 there were 150 students; girls and boys attended different classes. There were three professors, a tutor, and a lady who taught music and embroidery. The first permanent building, a $6,000 two-story stone structure, was opened the next year. The unpartitioned lower floor was used for chapel services and the boys attended classes upstairs, The girls remained in the old frame building, a mile away. The Reverend Rufus C. Burleson became president and the Reverend Horace Clark was appointed principal of the

These columns of the female department are reminders of Baylor's Independence origins.

female department in 1851. Three years later the enrollment was 190, there were four teachers in each department, and the physical plant was valued at $40,000. Burleson reported to the Baptist convention that, "The institution is supplied with a superior apparatus and a well-selected library, and the Honorable Sam Houston has tendered to the institution free use of his large and well-selected library ...."

Some of the conditions the student had to accept prior to registration were:

1st. You are not to use profane or obscene language about the college campus.
2nd. You are not to use ardent spirits, to treat others, or to visit dram shops or drinking houses.
3rd. You are not to carry about your person or keep in your room pistols, dirks, or any such weapons . . . .
4th. You are not to play at cards or any game of hazard.
5th. You are not to be out of your room after 9:00. You are not to engage in any nocturnal disorder or revelings.
6th. You are not to leave the institution without permission of the faculty.

Girls were to wear "bonnets of white straw, plainly trimmed with pink ribbon." Except for a plain breastpin, no jewelry was permitted. "Gay ribbons and extreme fashions" were prohibited.

Baylor's first degree was conferred upon Stephen Rowe in 1854. A three-story stone building for the girls was completed in 1857. In the following year the Bachelor of Laws degree was granted to 13 students. The best session at Independence was 1860, when 235 men and 140 women were enrolled, but examinations and commencement were not held in 1861 because, as Burleson put it, "the Civil War ... has suspended most of the best endowed colleges in the South." Mrs. Sarah Jane Scott, a teacher in the female department, wrote, "I want us women to learn to use the gun and the pistol well, and to ride well so that we can be ready if danger comes near home."

The war was not the only reason for the failure to hold commencement. Baylor had been developing into two institutions because of tensions between Clark and Burleson. Bad feelings had attended the removal of the boys to the new building while the girls kept the original structure. The old frame house had been in terrible condition when Baylor was founded, the walls consisting only of studs with boards covering the outside. After repairs the building sufficed only because everyone endured the same hardships. Burleson, who taught in the new building, had insisted that the girls remain apart. Clark believed Burleson was not sufficiently concerned with the women's needs, a judgment which was probably correct since Baylor's primary mission was the preparation of ministers, and it was assumed that girls need not be educated since their husbands would provide for them.

Clark, without Burleson's help, raised the necessary funds to build the three-story structure for the women. It was larger than the men's building and was probably the best educational facility in Texas. Burleson resented his subordinate's success. He believed that the building was more than the girls needed and that the donors would be unwilling to contribute again for other Baylor needs. When the plans were shown to him, Burleson deleted the third story; he was then enraged when Clark got a non-Baptist to contribute funds for the top floor and proceeded with the orginal design. Clark had acquired a building for his residence and dormitory use when he came to Baylor; this was the only dormitory the girls ever had at Independence.

Relations between the two departments were not improved by the scarcity of funds which kept the University in arrears on faculty salaries. Mrs. Sarah Scott, who was to receive $35 a month for teaching 65 girls seven hours a day and rooming with 14 of them, was not paid for months at a time. Clark's faculty believed expenses in the male department were always met first. Burleson seldom visited the women's building. By 1857 there had been so much friction between the two men that the

The women's department of Baylor University became Baylor Female College; it moved from Independence to Belton in 1886 and became Mary Hardin-Baylor College.

not merge; Baylor moved into the Waco University buildings. At the beginning of the 1886 session enrollment was 337, including 87 women. The new Baylor University conferred not only the Bachelor of Arts degree but also the Maid of Arts and Maid of Philosophy. Women were still supervised closely; governesses checked their outgoing mail and they wore uniform dresses, black in winter and white in the spring. Church and Sunday School were required. Study, except for the Bible, was not permitted on Sunday, and novels were never allowed.

Baylor Female College moved to Belton in 1886. Burleson and Clark were reconciled on an occasion when Clark was the baccalaureate speaker at Belton. After Clark resigned as president of Baylor Female College in 1871 he operated Clark's Academy in Houston. He became an Episcopalian and was made rector of the Corpus Christi Episcopal Church in 1880. Clark died in 1909 and Burleson in 1901.

Pat Neff Hall bears the name of the Texas governor who became president of Baylor University.

Nacogdoches University Was Chartered During the Republic

The founders of Nacogdoches University hoped to capitalize upon the unfortunate demise of the University of San Augustine, the first institution to be chartered by the Republic of Texas. The University of San Augustine had opened in 1842 and prospered, with the president, the Reverend Marcus Montrose, teaching the older students while they instructed the younger ones. San Augustine was calling itself "the Athens of Texas." Then after the University of San Augustine became affiliated with the Presbyterians, the Methodists founded Wesleyan College; a competition ensued which ruined both.

Nacogdoches and San Augustine had long been rivals, and as the San Augustine institutions failed, Nacogdoches citizens obtained a charter from the Republic. Montrose, a graduate of the University of Edinburgh, resigned from the University of San Augustine in 1845 and taught for one term at Nacogdoches University.

Founded by such distinguished citizens as General Thomas J. Rusk, Nacogdoches University had no church affiliation. Its initial endowment included 29,712 acres of land which had been granted to the municipality for the support of education in 1833, and $2,700 in cash and personal property. The university was first housed in a structure built by Colonel José de las Piedras for officers quarters. This adobe and frame building, called the Red House, had been General Rusk's home.

The University moved into Temperance Hall in the fifties and then finally settled at the site of the present Nacogdoches High School on Washington Square. A frame building was erected for the female department, and a two-story masonry structure was completed in 1859 for the men.

The departure of male students for Confederate service caused classes to be suspended, and the university buildings were used for hospital purposes during the Civil War. Union troops occupied them awhile in the reconstruction era. After the Nacogdoches University charter expired in 1870 the Sisters of Notre Dame used the buildings as a convent, and then the Nacogdoches Masonic Institute leased them. In 1887 Keachi College moved to the campus from Keachi, Louisiana, bringing a faculty of fifteen and offering Louisiana students free transportation to and from Shreveport. Keachi, which became Nacogdoches University, conferred the Bachelor of Arts, Maid of Arts, and Mistress of English Literature degrees.

When the second charter expired, in 1895, it was apparent that there was no need for a college at Nacogdoches. Some of the land had been sold to satisfy debts. Near the turn of the century disposition was made of the balance; the Washington Square property and building were given to the Nacogdoches school district. The 1859 brick building has been restored and currently houses a museum which is being developed by the Nacogdoches Federation of Women's Clubs.

Nacogdoches High School is located on the campus of old Nacogdoches University.

Southwestern's Predecessors Were Chartered by the Republic

Southwestern University was the successor of Rutersville College, McKenzie College, Soule University, and Wesleyan College. Rutersville grew out of the efforts of Martin Ruter, who responded to William Barret Travis' request for Methodist ministers. Ruter was raising funds for a university when he died. Land was purchased near La Grange, and Rutersville College was chartered and began instruction in 1840.

John McKenzie, a circuit-riding Methodist minister, began McKenzie College in a Red River County log cabin in November, 1841, offering only high school work at first. By the middle fifties it had nine professors, 300 students, and was Texas' largest college; it never recovered from the loss of students during the Civil War and closed in 1868.

Soule University opened at Chapell Hill, Washington County, in 1856, offering preparatory work to 95 students. Classes were suspended during the Civil War and twice in the reconstruction era because of yellow fever. Soule operated until 1888.

East Texas Methodists, in 1846, chartered Wesleyan Male and Female College as a rival of the Presbyterian University of San Augustine. After several misfortunes, including the shooting of its president, the University of San Augustine joined Wesleyan in 1847 to form the University of Eastern Texas, which did not long survive.

In 1873 five Methodist conferences chartered a new institution at Georgetown. President Mood, of Soule University, was made president of the new Texas University; in 1875, as the legislature was establishing the state university, the name became Southwestern University. Classes began in 1873, but there were few students. Georgetown, a village of 320 inhabitants, had no Methodist church. After the coming of the railroad, enrollment reached 109; fifty girls enrolled when the female department opened in 1878.

Until 1900 many Southwestern students were not capable of college work. Robert Hyer became president in 1898, and as high schools improved, he began dropping the preparatory courses. The campus was five blocks long, enclosed by a board fence, which was crossed by stiles. A bell in the three-story administration building sounded for classes, Sunday School, church, and prayer meetings. Hyer's daughter wrote, "In getting ready for any occasion it was time to get your hat on and start on your way when the first bell rang."

Southwestern produced three Rhodes Scholars at the turn of the century. As more students attended graduate school the university needed a record of grades. Professors had never reported them and resisted the copying of their grade books. One held out for two years.

By 1910 many thought Southwestern should be moved to a larger town. T.C.U. was leaving Waco, as Trinity had left Tehuacana. Enrollment was nearly a thousand, but Georgetown had reached a plateau; the location between Baylor and the state university, both flourishing, raised questions about Southwestern's future. Hyer supported a move to Dallas, but since litigation was threatened to enforce the charter requirement that Southwestern remain in Georgetown, a relocation was impossible. The Dallas idea persisted, and in 1915, when Southern Methodist University opened with 706 students, Dr. Hyer was its first president.

Southwestern University was the first permanently successful Methodist attempt to found a university in Texas.

Prince Carl Founded New Braunfels

In the early 19th century societies were formed to send unemployed Germans to New Zealand and the Americas. After an unsuccessful attempt was made to obtain Texas land in 1842, the Mainzer Adelsverein was founded at Mainz on March 25, 1844. Twenty-five princes and noblemen, headed by Prince Frederick of Prussia, contributed $80,000 to improve conditions there by sending destitute Germans abroad. Such an overseas population would constitute a new market for exports, and the organization would profit from land sales to the colonists.

In 1842, Henry Fisher, of Kassel, Germany, and Burchard Miller had been granted some four million acres between Texas' Llano and Colorado rivers. The Adelsverein bought their interest. The society offered 320 acres to heads of families and 160 acres to single men, titles to pass when the settler had built a house and had fifteen acres in cultivation. It would furnish domestic animals, food, and supplies, for which the colonist would pay after his second successive harvest.

Prince Carl, of Solms-Braunfels, the commissioner general, arriving in July, 1844, discovered that the Fisher-Miller grant was too far beyond the frontier for settlement. Another site had to be acquired, for colonists were on the way. In November and December, 439 arrived at Indian Point, renamed Carlshafen. In March the prince paid $1,111 for land on the Comal and Guadalupe rivers; New Braunfels was 165 miles from Galveston and 150 miles from the Fisher land.

Prince Carl mismanaged the inadequate funds furnished by the society and was $20,000 in debt when he asked to be relieved. His successor, Baron Ottfried von Meusebach, became John O. Meusebach as he reached Texas in May, 1845.

Prince Carl's manner had provoked animosities. Angered when an innkeeper put him at a table with other travelers, he was outraged when the landlord's wife set a place for herself at his separate table. A Texan was amused by watching a valet help Prince Carl into his trousers. An Austrian army officer, he kept a retinue of plumed and saber-rattling soldiers, who fired 21 rounds from the cannon to celebrate the birthday of his fiance, Princess Sophie of Salm-Salm. At the dedication of the Sophienburg the cannon was fired and the Austrian flag raised.

On his way inland Meusebach was accosted by Prince Carl's creditors. At New Braunfels he learned that the prince, anxious to marry Princess Sophie, had departed. Meusebach followed, found creditors detaining the prince at Galveston, and used up most of his funds freeing him.

The colonists endured severe hardships in beginning life at New Braunfels, but when Rutherford B. Hayes visited there he wrote:

> Those fairheaded Teutons have built in a short three years the most prosperous, singular, and interesting town in Texas. This is a German village of two or three thousand people at the junction of two of the most beautiful streams I ever saw, the Guadalupe and the Comal . . . . The water is so transparent that the fish seem to be hanging in the air.

On the site of Prince Carl's Sophienburg descendants of the original New Braunfels settlers erected this museum.

John O. Meusebach Founded Fredericksburg

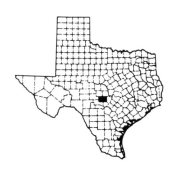

Baron Ottfried Hans Freiherr von Meusebach, born May 26, 1812, in Dillenburg, Nassau, studied law at the University of Bonn and was admitted to practice in 1836. Meusebach, the burgermeister of Anclam, was appointed by the Adelsverein to succeed Prince Carl of Solms-Braunfels. Upon coming to Texas, he became John O. Meusebach.

Meusbach found the enterprise insolvent, with most of the expense of moving the colonists inland still to be met. Because the Fisher-Miller grant was far beyond the frontier, New Braunfels had been founded, but it was filling up.

Meusebach chose a new site about 80 miles from New Braunfels and named it for Prince Frederick of Prussia. In December, 1845, three dozen men began building a road to Fredericksburg. Four months later 128 men, women and children went by ox cart to the 10,000 acre tract Meusebach had bought on credit. They arrived May 8, 1846, intending to stay in Fredericksburg only until they could claim their land in the Fisher-Miller tract. The colonists were given a half acre town lot and ten acres outside of Fredericksburg.

In the meantime more colonists were arriving, and Meusebach had no money to move them off the coast. About 4,000 landed in February, 1846; as they awaited transportation they sickened and starved. Survivors carried disease into the interior. At Fredericksburg 800 died—so many that bodies were sewn into sacks and funerals were no longer held. At the end of the year 700 colonists remained on the beach, although 180 hired wagons had been transporting settlers for four months.

By January, 1847, Fredericksburg's population was 500. Wilhelm Hermes remembered:

> The dearth of food-stuffs caused people to try substitutes. The sweet variety acorns from the live oak trees were not only used as a substitute for coffee, but for bread, too. The acorns were roasted, ground, and made into a dough, then baked.

Called El Sol Colorado by the Indians because of his reddish hair and beard, Meusebach negotiated a peace treaty with the Comanche in May, 1847. Two months later he resigned as commissioner general. Gillespie County was created, with Fredericksburg the capital, in 1848.

Meusebach was authorized by the state to issue land certificates in 1854. Earlier the insolvent Adelsverein had relinquished its rights. Heads of families were given 640 acres and single men 320, totaling some 1.7 million acres. Most colonists remained in New Braunfels and Fredericksburg and sold their western land.

While Meusebach was in Germany, in 1851, he was elected to the Texas Senate. He married Agnes Coreth, the Countess of Tyrol, at New Braunfels in 1852. He was forty; she was seventeen. Their eleven children were born at New Braunfels; after they were educated Meusebach moved to Loyal Valley, Mason County, where he died May 27, 1897. He was buried at Cherry Springs, Gillespie County.

Fredericksburg celebrated its fiftieth anniversary in 1896.

The Adelsverein Built the Coffee Mill Church

The first 120 settlers reached the Fredericksburg site on May 8, 1846. The men slept on the ground and women and children occupied the 29 ox carts while they built houses. The Adelsverein was to furnish food until crops were made, but funds were short, and more than 4,000 colonists had arrived. The Germans knew nothing of making bread from corn. Some died from eating pokeberry. Their physician incorrectly diagnosed illnesses he had not seen in Germany, which cost many lives.

The Adelsverein was to provide a church, for which a site was designated in the middle of the main street. Services were held beneath an oak tree until the Vereins Kirche, or community church, was built. It had the shape of an octagon, with the sides 18 feet square. The high, slanting roof above each side extended about 10 feet to form the base of an octagonal cupola with sides 10 feet square, which was topped by an octagonal roof seven feet high. Because it resembled a coffee mill the settlers called it Die Kaffemuehle. Women entered the north door and occupied half the church, while men used the south door and sat across the aisle.

The Reverend S. W. Basse preached the first sermon there; the congregation — mostly Protestant, but made up of all local denominations — called itself the Evangelical-Catholic Church. Catholics began meeting in John Leyendecker's home as missionary priests arrived. The Methodists left in 1849, and a few Lutheran families withdrew to form Zion Church in 1853.

The Vereins Kirche accomodated events such as the wedding of Catherine Zammert and Gottlieb Berrer in 1859. A procession from the bride's home included all the guests, with the men wearing bouquets. The first school was begun there even before the building was completed. Meusebach, fluent in five languages, urged support of education because "sensible persons are generally also good people."

In time there were churches, schoolhouses, and a courthouse to serve the many needs of the community. Soon after Fredericksburg's fiftieth anniversary 90 residents petitioned for removal of the Vereins Kirche. Finding the building, "being so shamefully desecrated by affording an offensive herding ground for cattle and horses contaminating the same, and being a disgraceful sight to the public besides it appearing from an examination that the sleepers and other parts have rotted and lost cohesion, rendering it unsafe and dangerous to enter same, and there being no protest against such action," the county commissioners ordered the structure removed, noting that the San Antonio-Mason road could then be straightened.

Anticipating the 1936 Texas Centennial, Fredericksburg constructed a replica of the Vereins Kirche some 200 feet from the original site. Built of limestone, with hand-hewn studs and rafters, the building contains the cornerstone of the original—which was lost for years and finally found in a chickenyard—and the bell from the old Vereins Kirche.

A replica of the Vereins Kirche, or Coffee Mill Church, was erected at Fredericksburg during the Texas Centennial celebration.

A Cross Stands Above Fredericksburg

John and Christine Binder Durst left Germany with their seven surviving children aboard the *Element* on August 25, 1846. They reached Fredericksburg in February, 1847. Durst received a town lot and acreage, as did his son, John Christian.

On John Christian Durst's land was a high hill; at the summit he found an old cross made of heavy timbers, which he raised. The Mount of the Holy Cross was an Indian landmark. Apparently Spanish missionaries—perhaps traveling between the San Sabá mission and San Antonio—erected the rough-hewn cross and met in council with Indians there.

In 1848 Father George Menzel erected a more substantial wooden cross, which was maintained through the years until St. Mary's parish duplicated it in concrete. Later, lights were installed to make the outline visible at night.

When the Easter Fires observance was begun, one of the stations was at the base of the cross. The celebration commemorates the Comanche treaty made by John O. Meusebach in 1847. As Meusebach's party rode out to meet the Comanche near present Menard, Indian scouts remained behind; they built fires on the hills around Fredericksburg as a signal that no troops followed.

Meusebach was ready to survey the Fisher grant in Comanche country. He told the chiefs:

> We have come a long way to smoke the peace pipe with the Comanche, and I have come with my people from across the big ocean . . . . I want to bring some of my people to the Llano River and make a settlement. We will plant corn and raise cattle and then our red brothers will have something to eat when the buffalo hunt fails.

For $1000 in goods the Comanche conveyed the land between the Llano and San Sabá rivers. By treaty the parties pledged "to use every exertion to keep up and even enforce peace and friendship between both the German and Comanche people and all other colonists and to walk in the white path always and forever."

Upon his return Meusebach learned that the Indian bonfires on the hills had worried those at Fredericksburg. He was told of some frightened children asking their mother about the fires. Not wanting to distress them with the truth, the woman revised an old German myth, but instead of fairies burning dead growth to make way for the new, she told of rabbits coloring Easter eggs; they were boiling wildflowers with the eggs over great fires. Meusebach, pleased, declared that the Easter rabbit's fires would be kindled annually for so long as the Comanche treaty was unbroken.

Since the hundreth Easter Fires observance in 1947 there has been an annual pageant in which more than 400 citizens participate. It begins with kindergarten children gathering flowers for the nests into which the rabbit will place Easter eggs, while the evening bells of the churches sound and fires are built on the Mount of the Holy Cross and the other hills surrounding the town by fourth and fifth generation descendants of the settlers of Fredericksburg.

The illuminated successor of a heavy timber cross apparently used by Spanish missionaries overlooks Fredericksburg.

The Nimitz Was the Place to Stay in West Texas

Charles Nimitz, of Bremen, Germany, became a merchant seaman at the age of fourteen. An original settler of Fredericksburg, he married Sophie Mueller in April, 1848. After serving with the rangers, in 1852 he opened the Nimitz Hotel which was, for a generation, the only first-class inn between San Antonio and San Diego, California. The orginal hotel was a single story, four-room, frame structure. A native stone addition housed a saloon and increased the rooms to thirty; a final expansion, about 1880, added fifteen rooms and gave the hotel its distinctive riverboat appearance.

Herman Toepperwein, a Nimitz descendant, wrote:

> Inside a spacious lobby, guests found a bar to the right, a neat little parlor to the left with windows opening on Main Street. Beyond the parlor were rooms and the living quarters for the Nimitz family (there were twelve children; nine lived to adulthood); immediately outside this wing grew a quiet, formal flower garden that was Mother Nimitz's pride and joy. Adjoining the lobby was a high-ceilinged, combination casino-theatre-dance hall, with a balcony running along the left side and rear. From the balcony, passages led to rooms on the second floor and to those in the Steamboat section (the most desirable ones, since they caught the most breeze). Also on the left side of the big hall a door opened into the most famous dining room on the frontier.

Nimitz had to provide most of the hotel's needs. Behind the main building was a smokehouse, vegetable garden, and orchard. He had a brewery, and beer was stored in the basement. The hotel was the social center for soldiers at forts Concho, McKavett, Martin Scott, and Mason. Nimitz offered not only lodging but a bathhouse with hot water and tin bathtubs. Among his guests were generals Philip Sheridan, James Longstreet, and Robert E. Lee, the sculptress Elisabet Ney, and President Rutherford B. Hayes. A Gillespie County historian wrote of the hotel at Christmas:

> A cedar tree decorated with wax candles adorned the lobby and the climax always came on New Years Eve. People came from far and near to dance the Schottische, the reel, and to polka until midnight . . . .

The host was a good companion; Nimitz and his cronies regularly played practical jokes on each other. His friends circulated a story that a guest died at the hotel and his relatives, who lived far away, asked that the embalmed body be sent to them; since there was no mortician, Captain Nimitz smoke-cured him and shipped him home.

In 1861 the German counties favored the Union, but Nimitz remained a Democrat. He was captain of the Gillespie Rifles and was the Confederate conscription officer. After the war he boarded destitute friends until they could begin new lives. He died in 1911 at the age of 84. A remodeling in 1926 gave the hotel its present appearance; closed after 116 years, it now houses the Admiral Nimitz Center, named for the captain's grandson, Chester.

The old Nimitz Hotel houses the Admiral Nimitz Center, honoring the grandson of the hotel's founder.

The Norwegians Settled at Brownsboro

Norwegians had been interested in the United States since Kleng Peerson's 1821 visit; he encouraged emigration and later established colonies in Missouri, Iowa, and Illinois. Johann Reierson, the editor of *Christianssanposten*, visited midwestern Norwegian settlements in 1843 and wrote a guide for emigrants.

In March, 1845, Reierson brought settlers to New Orleans. Preferring a warm climate, he bought a certificate for unoccupied land in Texas. Some of his group chose Missouri; Reierson brought the others to Nacogdoches, where he wrote of a ball, "I looked around in amazement at this company of high-ranking personages . . . but could not discover the least trace of that superciliousness that usually characterizes our upper classes and betrays itself even in their poorly disguised condescension." Reierson's settlement at Brownsboro, which he called Normandy, was Texas' first Norwegian colony; John Nordvoe, of Norway, had settled near Dallas earlier.

There was much sickness and disappointment at first, but the settlers' morale and health improved and their letters brought more Norwegians to Texas.

Johann Reierson moved west to Four Mile Prairie, leaving his father, Ole, behind. In 1849 Ole Reierson wrote to an old friend:

> All the children, with the exception of Ole Andreas, from whom I have heard nothing for two years, live well and have good incomes, each in his position, and none of us has any reason to regret our decision to leave our fatherland . . . . Johann lives further up on a prairie thirty-five English miles from my place . . . . All this land is the most fertile plowland that brings forth all kinds of seeds without any manure . . . . One lives here very easily and comfortably when one has first won over the initial difficulties with regard to house building and land clearing . . . . Cattle and pigs show considerable yearly increase, as they feed themselves; there is no expense in looking after the cattle as they move freely in the forest fields and return by themselves each evening. In every regard one is free and one's own master. There is no authority one needs to crawl for or fear in humility, only obey the laws, and these are alike for all, and not hard . . . .
>
> Of news I have none, only that wherever people gather the talk turns to California, gold mining and gold digging . . . . People that heretofore lived as, and were, farmers, leave their farm properties and neither sow nor harvest. Now I have nothing more to tell you . . . . But if there still is something lacking and that I miss, it is some Norwegian friends and acquaintances . . . . It would gladden me if some brave, righteous family found it possible to leave Norway and move here.

The Normandy colony was never large, and many followed Johann Reierson to Four Mile Prairie; later some moved from both places to Bosque County, where Kleng Peerson settled in 1854. Only sixteen Norwegian families remained at Brownsboro and seventeen at Four Mile Prairie in 1869, the year of Peerson's death. Johann Reierson had died during the Civil War.

The Tergerson House was built near Brownsboro by Norwegians who came to Texas with Johann Reierson.

A Norwegian Lady Wrote of Early Texas

Elise Tvede, of Danish parentage but raised in Norway, was married for a time to Svend Foyn, the founder of the Norwegian whaling industry. When Johann Reierson left for Texas she edited his magazine. She emigrated in 1847, stopped at Brownsboro, and settled on Four Mile Prairie in Van Zandt County. She married Wilhelm Woerenskjold, who was killed in 1866 at Prairieville.

Her letters constitute an invaluable contemporary account of life in early Texas. She thought that Four Mile Prairie "closely resembles Denmark and is very pretty. Brownsboro, on the other hand, is more like Norway, as the land is very hilly and has high ridges and large pine woods." But Texas was much easier to farm:

> In Norway if a person wants to turn a piece of unbroken land into a field it will cost him much labor . . . . Here a person barely needs to fence and plow the land and it is ready to be sown (this is true only on the prairie; the forest land must be cleared of brush and large trees must be girdled . . . . The wheat is simply placed on the ground and trampled out by horses or oxen. Much grain, of course, being lost in the process . . . . Corn is the most common crop and cornmeal is generally used for baking. It is well-liked by those who are used to it, but I must say frankly that I find it to be a poor type of bread.

Of the wild animals she wrote:

> To be sure, quite a few beasts of prey are found here. There are panthers (a kind of tiger the size of a dog but shaped like a cat), bears, wolves, foxes, opossums, skunks, several types of snakes, and alligators in the lakes and rivers. But there is enough food for all the animals so they do not need to attack human beings . . . . Snakes can be a nuisance and they crawl clear up to the second story, especially a type called the chicken snake because it eats chickens and eggs which it swallows whole. The reason for its intrusion into houses is that the hens usually have their nests under the beds and up in the lofts.
>
> So far as the Texans are concerned, a person has nothing to fear from them unless he gets into trouble with them—then they are really much too prone to avenge every real or fancied insult with a bullet or a stab. But I am certain there is no land in the world where a person has less reason to fear assault or robbery than here, for such things are unheard of . . . . In all business dealings with them, one must guard against being "taken by the nose" because they look upon cheating about as people in Norway regarded smuggling during my childhood.
>
> I mentioned above that Americans are inclined to cheat. From this a person might conclude that they would also be given to stealing, but this is so far from being the truth that I am sure there are few countries where one's possessions are as safe as they are here . . . .

Through the years she saw Four Mile Prairie decline as Norwegians moved to Bosque County. Her son, Thorvald, died in childhood; of the others she wrote shortly before her death at Hamilton, in 1895, "I have two sons, both married to Americans, who, as well as my grandchildren, do not understand Norwegian."

Elise Woerenskjold edited Johann Reierson's magazine in Norway and then settled in Texas.

The Penitentiary Was Located at Huntsville

In the last days of the Republic sentiment was building for less severe punishments and the establishment of a penitentiary. The penal code prescribed the death penalty for arson, burglary, rape, murder, and robbery. The penalty for theft of $20 or more was 39 lashes on the bare back and branding of the right hand with the letter "T". A penitentiary authorized in 1842 was never established. The first effort for a penal system had been made in 1829 by the legislature of Coahuila y Texas in approving establishment of panoptic — designed so guards could see into the cells without being seen — prisons; private firms would build and maintain them and would be entitled to the prisoners' labor. The plan failed when no one offered to build the prisons.

In 1848, the legislature adopted a penal code requiring penitentiary confinement. A commission was to locate the penitentiary; the buildings were to be erected with hired labor. Earlier plans had the convicts doing the construction. The commissioners chose Huntsville as the site. They paid $15 for two tracts of 418 acres, and $470 for 94 acres of timber. They also took deeds for building rock. Henderson Yoakum, lawyer, historian, and a director of the penitentiary, donated a hundred acres of timber rights. Abner Cook, an experienced builder, was made the superintendent.

By April, 1849, a building to house a dozen convicts was under construction. A fifteen-foot wall was to enclose three prisons; one would have 144 cells and one 86 cells and two dungeons. The third, with 36 cells, was for women; its cells were larger than those for men. A two-story building was provided for the administration. Workshops were to be housed along the walls. Construction was slowed by bad weather, sightseers, shortages of materials, and difficulties in hiring workers.

The first convict, William Samson—with a three year sentence from Fayette County—arrived October 1. Because the new penal code applied only to offenses committed after December 31, 1848, the time consumed in trial and the usual delays kept any convicts from being forwarded in the first nine months. Samson had been convicted through the efforts of the vigilante group which arrested him . Committed to jail, before the trial he made a written confession to the vigilantes. He was then indicted for larceny and tried and sentenced by the district court.

Texas population was only 151,000, and about three convicts reached Huntsville each month. To help make the penitentiary self-supporting a textile mill was begun in 1854. During the Civil War, since there were not enough prisoners to make the cloth the Confederacy needed free labor was used in the mill and officials were permitted to borrow Arkansas, Missouri, and Louisiana convicts.

In 1863 some captured Union sailors and army officers were imprisoned at Huntsville. Colonel Duganne, a prisoner of war incarcerated elsewhere, wrote:

> In this penitentiary 168 convicts were confined at hard labor. . . . On weekdays the (convicts) were called to work at 5 a.m. and relieved at six in the evening. The cells of this state prison were not inviting dormitories, being overrun with cockroaches and overbrooded by mosquitos . . . . Various local entertainment assisted the time to pass. On one day a convict would be placed in the stocks; another morning ushered in some negro, accused of attempting to kill his owner while the latter was flogging him. Once General Houston came—he resided near the penitentiary—and talked "secesh" to our officers. But Colonel Caruthers, the superintendent, did not keep our Federals in convict quarters very long. He fitted up a large upper room . . . and gave our officers possession of it.

The main entrance to the penitentiary at Huntsville is located beneath the clock.

About the close of May . . . a message arrived from Governor Lubbock, the Texan executive, expressing fears that the presence of our Yankees at Huntsville might attract a Federal expedition against the important place. The brave governor said the Yankees must be removed. The manufacture of 5,000 yards of cotton cloth per diem, with sundry other items of Texan fabrication by penitentiary machinery, must not be jeopardized by Yankee Jonahs. So, presently it transpired, toward the end of June, that our prisoners were led out of Huntsville prison and then deported to Camp Groce . . . .

In July, 1871, the penitentiary was leased for a 15-year term. The lessee was to pay the state $5,000 per annum for the first five years, $10,000 for each of the second five years, and $20,000 a year thereafter. The prison population was 906 men and 21 women in 1873. About 250 convicts were laying railroad track—including Kiowa chiefs Satanta and Big Tree—and the others made cloth, doors, furniture, wagons, shoes, and clothing at Huntsville. The leasing plan was abandoned in 1883 in favor of a system wherein the state housed, fed, and transported convicts and sold their service to private contractors. Next the state tried farming on the shares; private land was farmed for 60% of the cotton and 50% of the sugar cane. The state then began buying land for convicts to farm. A Rusk iron foundry was operated for a number of years, shipping its products over its own railroad. The iron works and railroad were sold in 1920 after losing more than $2 million.

Some questionable transactions occurred in the acquisition of farms, such as the payment of $13.75 an acre for Ramsey Prison Farm land that had cost the seller $5 an acre two years earlier. A probe showed that the Darrington and Retrieve farms had cost far too much and were occasionally flooded. Scandal involving the prison system was a regular occurrence, as were legislative investigations.

In 1928 Governor Pat Neff appointed Lee Simmons to a committee which began a campaign against corruption and mismanagement. There were then eleven prison farms with 73,000 acres of land. The cattle operation was typical of the graft the committee discovered. The prison system brand was a five-pointed star, and it was found that dozens of landowners near the prison farms were using star brands with the addition of a letter or numeral, a practice which explained the failure of prison herds to increase.

There were 5,000 convicts in the system, and escapes were a regular occurrence; sixty-five convicts got away in one month. In 1930 Simmons became superintendent of the prison system and began rectifying some of the conditions alluded to by Governor Dan Moody when he said, "If I had a dog that I thought anything of, I wouldn't want him kept in the Texas penitentiary under present conditions." Simmons' five year tenure provided the foundation for the Texas Department of Corrections.

The last resting place of thousands of convicts, most of the headstones are penitentiary-made and bear no names, only numbers. Captain Joe Byrd was once the state executioner.

A Fort Was Built on the Upper Trinity

Annexation transferred responsibility for Texas frontier defense to the federal government. In addition, the United States had promised to keep raiding parties out of Mexico. A line of forts seemed to be the solution to both problems; one outpost would be located in present Tarrant County to protect north Texas.

Tarrant County's first permanent settlement, Lonesome Dove, had been established in 1845 near modern Grapevine; Dr. D.D. Tidwell noted that, "not a Protestant church stood between the Lonesome Dove Church and the Pacific Ocean." During the Mexican War Colonel Middleton Tate Johnson quartered his troops at Johnson's station, three miles south of present Arlington, where he later commanded a ranger company.

Johnson's aid was sought by Major Ripley Arnold in locating the easternmost of a chain of forts extending to the Rio Grande. General William Jenkins Worth wanted the post to be near the confluence of the Clear and West forks of the Trinity. Simon Farrar, who was there when the site was chosen, wrote:

> We passed through . . . a wild, beautiful country inhabited only by Indians, wild mustang horses, innumerable deer, wolves and wild turkey . . . . About three o'clock in the evening we halted in the valley east of where Fort Worth now stands and killed a deer for supper . . . . Next morning Colonel Johnson and Major Arnold . . . started to locate the barracks. We went west until we reached the point where the Court House now stands, there halted and reviewed the scenery from all points and I thought it the most beautiful and grand country that the sun ever shone on and while we were at that place, in view of all advantages of a natural point of defense, and our late experience at Monterrey, wherein the strategic action of General Worth had so terribly defeated the Mexicans, we there, in honor of that grand old hero, named the point Fort Worth.

The land was owned by Johnson, who agreed to the Army's use for as long as necessary. The flag was raised on June 6, 1849, as the post was founded by Ripley and his 25 enlisted men. Fort Worth's log buildings were situated around a quadrangle bounded by present Houston, Throckmorton, Bluff, and Weatherford streets. On the bluff above the Trinity was a row of small buildings housing laundresses, bakehouses, quartermaster's stores, and a mess hall. The next row consisted of barracks, kitchen, and guardhouse. Across the 250-foot parade ground were three houses for the officers. Two rows of stables extended across the north end of the quadrangle, and a hospital and adjutant's office occupied the south side. The fort was not stockaded.

The frontier advanced rapidly. By the time Fort Worth was abandoned on September 17, 1853, Dallas County's population was 2,700, and Birdville, the seat of Tarrant County, had about fifty residents. Settlers moved into the vacated army buildings.

Major Arnold was killed at Fort Graham by the post surgeon eleven days before Fort Worth's abandonment.

General Worth ordered the establishment of a fort on the Trinity River where the Tarrant County courthouse now stands.

Lindheimer was the Father of Texas Botany

Ferdinand Lindheimer was one of many gifted men who came to Texas because of political unrest in the German states. Born into a wealthy family May 21, 1801, at Frankfort-on-the-Main, Lindheimer attended the University of Bonn and taught at George Bunsen's Frankfort school. After a riot in 1833, the school was closed and six teachers were charged with sedition. Lindheimer fled to the United States. After becoming the manager of a Mexican plantation in 1834 he began collecting specimens of plants and insects.

Lindheimer came to Texas to help the colonists against Santa Anna but reached San Jacinto the day after the battle. While truck-farming near Houston, he began to wonder whether he could make a living from botany. Texas plants seemed to represent a transition between Mexican species and those in the United States. Professor Asa Gray of Harvard College encouraged him; Lindheimer was to collect and mount specimens for $8 per hundred plants.

In March, 1843, Lindheimer began his collecting at Galveston; these specimens are in the collections of the Missouri Botanical Gardens at St. Louis. Ferdinand Roemer described Lindheimer's methods in this fashion:

> He bought a two-wheeled covered cart with a horse, loaded it with a pack of pressing-paper and a supply of the most indispensible provisions, namely flour, coffee, and salt, then set forth into the wilderness, armed with his rifle and with no other companion than his two hunting dogs, while he occupied himself with collecting and pressing plants. He depended for his subsistence mainly upon his hunting, often passing whole months at a time without seeing a human being.

After collecting near Houston he worked Waller and Austin counties. In 1844 he collected west of the Brazos; while living with the Robert Klebergs at Cat Springs he learned of the Adelsverein's colonization project. Lindheimer accompanied the first colonists to the New Braunfels site. There he built a house and prospected the area for botanical specimens. The Indians did not bother him, believing he was a mighty medicine man who used the plants in magic potions. He collected specimens until 1852 when he became the editor of the *Neu Braunfelser Zeitung*. His interest in botany continued; a score of species were named for him.

Lindheimer was active in the building of New Braunfels. The minutes of the Comal County Commissioners Court reflect his 1856 offer to publish in German, for $3.50, a hundred copies of the new road law. The county clerk was ordered to be sure that each road overseer who was not fluent in English had a copy. Although unsympathetic to slavery, after secession Lindheimer urged his readers to help the Confederacy bring the war to a rapid conclusion. On New Braunfels' twenty-fifth anniversary Lindheimer wrote, "a no more fortunate union of the national characteristics of two peoples can be sought than those of the Germanic races who, after fifteen hundred years of separation, again meet on American soil to build Freedom's Temple, for the foundation of which the cornerstone was laid in their hearts long before Herman's time."

Ferdinand Lindheimer built his New Braunfels home while collecting Texas plants and editing a newspaper.

A Cemetery Was Established for the State

The desire to honor General Edward Burleson brought the State Cemetery into existence. A militia colonel in both Missouri and Tennessee, Burleson had moved to Austin's second colony in 1830. He commanded a regiment at San Jacinto, was congressman and vice president of the Republic, and served Texas in many other capacities. At his death, December 26, 1851, he was president pro tempore of the Texas Senate. A joint legislative committee arranged for burial on Austin land belonging to Andrew J. Hamilton. Later the property was acquired by the state for use as a cemetery.

By 1861 only Supreme Court Justice Abner Lipscomb and State Senator Forbes Britton had been interred there, but during the Civil War Confederate Senator John Hemphill, and generals Hugh McLeod, Ben McCulloch, and William Scurry were buried, bringing to seven the total number of graves. The first reburial was that of General Albert Sidney Johnston in 1867. Few men in American history have been so idolized as Johnston, killed at Shiloh five years before and buried at New Orleans. Because Johnston had commanded the Texas Army and had been their Secretary of War Texans intended to move his body to Austin after the war. In late 1866 the legislature sent representatives to New Orleans to make the arrangements.

In January, 1867, the New Orleans *Picayune* reported the disinterment. Former Confederate generals Beauregard, Bragg, Buckner, Hood, Longstreet, and others were all pallbearers. Although a program had been planned at Galveston, General Charles Griffin, the federal commander, forbade any funeral procession. An appeal to General Philip Sheridan was fruitless. Sheridan wrote, "I have too much regard for the memory of the brave men who died to preserve our Government to authorize Confederate demonstrations over the remains of anyone who attempted to destroy it."

Texans were outraged. The body lay in state for a day and thousands of citizens formed a procession behind the hearse as it crossed Galveston. By the time the funeral train reached there, Houston's citizenry was defiant. Ignoring Griffin's orders, houses were draped from roof to ground with crepe streamers. For two days the coffin, surrounded by flowers and portraits of Lee, Jackson, and Davis, was visited by mourners. The military warned against a demonstration, but most Houstonians accompanied Johnston's remains to the train which was to take the body to Austin. A newspaperman reported, "The bells are tolling. The solemn cortege is one mile in length. Five hundred ladies and little girls are on foot in the procession. No military officials are seen on the streets." In Austin, after similar ceremonies, Johnston was laid to rest at the State Cemetery. In 1901 the legislature appropriated $10,000 for a monument; Elisabet Ney executed a recumbent statue of Johnston and a canopy was built for its protection.

Stephen F. Austin was re-interred at the State Cemetery in 1910, where he rests beside such Texans as Bigfoot Wallace, Francis Lubbock, Robert M. Williamson, and Walter Prescott Webb.

The tomb of General Albert Sidney Johnston is a landmark of the State Cemetery.

Elizabeth Crockett Followed Her Husband to Texas

David Crockett, an early Jackson supporter, lost his congressional seat by opposing Andrew Jackson's election to the United States Senate. His reaction was to send word to his Tennessee constituents that "they can go to hell, and I'm going to Texas." Crockett, born in Hawkins County, Tennessee, August 17, 1786, married Polly Finley when he was nineteen and moved to Lincoln County. He fought under Jackson in the Creek War of 1813. Two years later his wife died, leaving him with three small children, John, who was later a Tennessee congressman, William, and Polly. He then married Elizabeth Patton, a widow with two children, and moved 80 miles west to Giles County. There he was a justice of the peace and legislator. Once again he moved westward to new country, this time to the junction of the Obion and the Mississippi rivers. He killed 105 bears within less than a year, and was again sent to the legislature; during this time he earned the Jacksonians' animosity. Through the years his legend had been growing. He ran for Congress as a joke, then became serious about it; he was defeated the first time, but then succeeded and took his seat in 1827. He was defeated for re-election in 1830, won again in 1832, and after the voters turned him out in 1835, in exasperation he headed for Texas as Haley's comet paid its regular visit and the Texas revolution began. Mrs. Crockett was to follow as soon as her husband found a place to his liking. From San Augustine, on January 9, 1836, he wrote to two of his children, stating that he would be entitled to a headright of 4,438 acres and expected to settle on Choctaw Bayou near Red River.

Eighteen years after David Crockett died at the Alamo, Mrs. Crockett came to Texas with her son, Robert, and his family. They lived in Ellis County for two years, then moved onto 320 acres in present Hood County which were deeded to Mrs. Crockett by the state. She never claimed the headright to which she was entitled by virtue of her husband's wartime service. Elizabeth Crockett, born in Buncombe County, North Carolina, May 22, 1788, died in Hood County, January 31, 1860. She was buried at the Acton Cemetery. The State of Texas commissioned a statue, which was placed over her grave in 1913. This "smallest state cemetery in Texas" has the graves of Mrs. Crockett, her son, Robert Patton Crockett, and his wife, Matilda Porter Crockett.

Elizabeth Crockett was buried at Acton twenty-four years after her husband died at the Alamo.

Panna Maria Was the First Polish Colony

Thousands of Poles emigrated because of the partitioning of Poland, the loss of Polish independence, natural disasters, and famine. The first colony to come to the United States was urged to do so by a Polish Conventual Franciscan missionary, the Reverend Leopold Moczygemba, who was ministering to the Germans, Alsatians, and French at New Braunfels, Castroville, and San Antonio. His letters to kinsmen promised a life in Texas free of the oppression they had always known.

Father Moczygemba bought land upon which to locate the settlers from John Twohig in 1854, the year Karnes County was organized. The first 150 Poles reached Galveston by sailing ship from Bremen, Germany, in December and arrived at the Panna Maria site on Christmas Eve; midnight mass was said beneath a great oak tree. The settlers camped out that winter while they built homes. They had walked the 200 miles from Galveston, with hired Mexican ox carts bringing their possessions and the cross from their former church. Seven hundred more came in 1855, and a third group arrived the next year. Many left Panna Maria after a short time for San Antonio and Victoria and to found new towns.

Construction of a new church was begun in 1855 and completed in September, 1856. The stone church, 70 feet long and 36 feet wide, was the first built by Poles in the new world. Twenty-one years later it was so badly damaged by lightning that a new building was needed; the present church, finished in February, 1878, was enlarged and remodeled in 1937.

The first Polish school in the United States, St. Joseph's, at Panna Maria, was completed May 15, 1868. It was a stone building, with classrooms downstairs and priests' quarters above. As was the case in building the church, members of the parish furnished locally-quarried stone, other materials, and much of the labor. The priests taught for a time and were succeeded by lay teachers and sisters of various orders.

The 1860 census of Karnes County reveals an absence of business and professional men at Panna Maria, causing Jacek Przygoda to write, "The German and Czech peasants had a jump on the Poles, timewise. They were also fortunate to have in their midst a number of well-educated leaders from their own native land. The Texas Poles had to do things by themselves." That 1860 census reflected a Polish citizenry of some 400 out of a population of 2,171. Ten years later the county had only 1,705 residents. Some of that loss was due to Polish settlers moving away. A traveler wrote of Panna Maria in 1857:

> One or two hundred arrived on the ground in February, 1855, seven hundred more in the autumn, and some five hundred additional in 1856. The site was chosen . . . without discrimination, and the spot has proved so unhealthy as to induce a desertion of about one-half of the survivors, who have made a settlement in the eastern upper corner of Medina County.

The 1970 population of Panna Maria was 96.

IMMACULATE CONCEPTION
CATHOLIC CHURCH
PANNA MARIA TEXAS

OLDEST POLISH CATHOLIC
COLONY IN THE U.S.
FOUNDED DECEMBER 24, 1854

The first Polish colonists attended mass under a Panna Maria live oak tree on Christmas Eve, 1854.

The Camels Were Quartered at Camp Verde

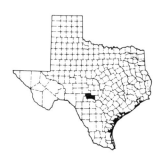

A major problem in the middle of the 19th century was that of communications with the western states. Eventually there would be a transcontinental railroad, but until that could be built another form of transport was needed. The Army was particularly concerned.

In 1853 Jefferson Davis became Franklin Pierce's Secretary of War. Years before, while he was a Senator from Mississippi, Major Henry Wayne had talked to him about the use of camels in the southwest. Now Davis recommended that experiments be conducted in connecting Texas and California by camel transport; in March, 1855, Congress appropriated $30,000 for that purpose.

Major Wayne was sent to North Africa aboard the Navy storeship *Supply*, commanded by Lt. David D. Porter, to get the camels. The Mohammed Pasha at Tunis gave Wayne, as a gift to the American president, two "gimels." Wayne wrote Davis that there were three kinds of gimel, the Bactrian, which had two humps and was a carrier of freight; the one-humped dromedary, for riding and racing; and the booghdee or Tinlu, which was a hybrid of the other two and, like a mule, could not reproduce itself. By February 11, 1856, Wayne had 33 camels aboard ship. The sailors, knowing that Pehlavans were trained to wrestle each other, taught the youngest camel, Uncle Sam, some wrestling holds. After he hurt several of them the sailors let him alone. One camel died on the voyage but two were born. The camels were unloaded at Powder Horn, Texas, on May 13.

Wayne had brought three handlers with him, Greek George, Mico the Arab, and a Turk named Hadji Ali — which, in Texan, was pronounced Hi Jolly. Residents of Indianola were impressed by the strength of the camels, as they handled 500-pound loads with ease. The sight and scent of the camels frightened horses and mules, and a Victoria resident reported that a horseman would be sent out ahead to warn of the camels' approach. After letting the animals rest and recover from the voyage, Wayne took them out of Indianola on June 4. They reached San Antonio fourteen days later. Mrs. Robert Clark wrote that as he passed through Victoria:

> Major Wayne presented to my mother, Mrs. Mary Shirkey, some of the hair which he had clipped from one of the camels, and she knitted a pair of socks for the President of the United States, Franklin Pierce . . . . When the hair was presented to her the odor was most terrible.

Wayne hoped that the first camels would be used for breeding purposes only. They were not accustomed to the country, but their offspring would be sufficiently adjusted to be worked. Wayne feared that working the imported herd would simply destroy them and prove nothing. Introduction of the camel to this hemisphere was to be the object, and he believed, "to achieve this will require time, five years at least." If Wayne's plans were followed, "I have little doubt that in ten years the race will be well spread through Texas, whence it can be carried to any part of the continent." His suggestions were ignored; Davis believed testing of the camels for military service should not wait. Feasibility could be determined with the initial group, and if the experiment were successful more could be imported and bred.

The camels arrived at Camp Verde, 60 miles northwest of San Antonio, on August 26. Corrals such as those the camels had always used were built; the walls were 16 feet high and constructed of stone, timber, and adobe. Camp Verde had been

The Camp Verde officers' quarters have been converted into apartments.

established seven weeks earlier on the north bank of Verde Creek. In early tests Wayne reported that:

> ... 6 transported over the same ground and distance the weights of two six-mule wagons and gained on them 42½ hours in time. Remember, moreover, that the keep of a camel is about the same as that of a mule ....

A dromedary carrying more than 300 pounds of supplies for a troop pursuing Indians had to be restrained to keep it from outdistancing the horses.

Wayne left Camp Verde and the experiment in January, 1857. The Navy landed another 41 camels that month. They were taken to Camp Verde. Forty more were imported by an English lady the next year; they were kept near Houston and always generated great excitement when Arab handlers took them into town. Twenty-five of the government camels were sent to California in the middle of 1857.

Colonel Robert E. Lee watched the testing of the camels with interest. In May, 1859, a contingent of 24 camels and 24 mules left San Antonio for Fort Davis, in the Big Bend country. All were heavily laden. The camels performed well, but another test was needed. Lee ordered another journey in May, 1860, through the roughest part of the Big Bend. With 20 camels and 15 pack mules Lieutenant William Echols and about 35 soldiers almost died of thirst, but Lee was convinced of the superiority of camels as beasts of burden.

John B. Floyd, Davis' successor as Secretary of War, asked Congress for 1,000 more camels. By their use he hoped to establish the route to California so well that when the transcontinental railroad was built it would follow the same course through the South; probably for that very reason Congress did not grant the request. The camel project languished. While the climate was appropriate, the ground was hard on their feet; they were used to sandy country and the rocks caused them difficulty.

As the southern states were beginning to secede, in January, 1861, Colonel C. A. Waite, the commander at Camp Verde, ordered preparations for resistance. He thought Camp Verde the least defensible site he had ever seen; the public property there, including 53 camels, was worth $20,000. General David Twiggs sent additional soldiers, but on March 1 Federal troops abandoned the post. The Confederates used the camels to haul cotton, swinging a bale from either side of the animals. When the war ended, 44 camels remained at Camp Verde.

Bethel Coopwood bought some of the camels, sold five to the Ringling Circus, and started a camel transport and mail service into Mexico. Of those taken to California before the war, some were seen roaming that country by gold miners, one as late as 1891. In that same year a Victoria physician, hunting for some burros near Kingsville, Texas, saw two camels wandering around. Of the herders, Greek George became George Allen when he received his citizenship papers in California. Hi Jolly, who took the name Phillip Tedro, is buried at Quartzsite, Arizona, beneath a marker shaped like a pyramid and with a camel figure on the top.

At Camp Verde the Army carried out its camel experiment.

Goliad Has a Hanging Tree

On the Goliad courthouse square stands an oak tree whose bloody past is certain although the identities of those hanged there have been lost to history; some were victims of the "Cart War" of the 1850's.

As the slavery controversy continued, antagonisms toward those of Mexican extraction grew because of the assumption that they were helping runaway slaves escape into Mexico. Mexican-American families were driven out of Austin, Seguin, and Columbus. In 1857 Mexicans were prohibited from entering Uvalde County without a passport.

The Goliad city council appointed patrols to supervise the slaves; one found away from where he was supposed to be was subject to 25 lashes on the bare back; one caught with a deadly weapon could receive 39 lashes. Slaves from nearby farms could visit Goliad on Sunday afternoons only if they had families there, and they could not remain after sundown.

In that time there were Mexican ox cart drivers hauling goods from Indianola to San Antonio. To other freighters their offense was two-fold: they were suspected of aiding runaway slaves, and they charged less than the Texans. Since merchants wanted to pay as little as possible for shipping, the cartmen were ruining the other freighters. Guerrilla warfare broke out near Goliad. A secret organization was formed and masked men began attacking the carts, seizing their cargos and killing the drivers. The violence led to assaults on other freighters, too; General David Twiggs, the commander at San Antonio, had to assign troops to guard Army supplies in transit.

The reaction of the cartmen was to bypass Goliad. Frustrated members of the secret society plundered the homes of Goliad residents who had no part in the controversy. These victims appealed to the governor for help. In addition, Mexico's minister at Washington protested, charging that by October, 1857, 75 Mexicans had been killed. The State Department complained to Governor E. M. Pease, who began an investigation and asked for legislation. When the legislature was slow to act, the governor sent rangers; by that time Goliad had solved its own problem. Influential men, who had ignored the outrages at first, took charge; a citizen reported, "Judge Lynch did it with his little rope."

Jim Pettus, who lived in Goliad, wrote:

> The most malicious times that I remember came during the cart cutting war, but all that is a matter of history now, of course; yet the pages of history and the cold slabs on landmarks are but tame reminders to one who has actually witnessed the horror, destruction, and desolation; to one who has heard men curse and pray alternately before the hangman's noose tightened about their necks. To me, the old oak tree in front of the courthouse is only one of the many reminders of a day that I might well want to forget, for there, after having been assigned to guard two prisoners all night at the courthouse, I saw them hanged.

The ox cart drivers went back to Mexico, and the war ended.

This tree on the Goliad courthouse square was the gallows for a number of Cart War participants.

Charles Schreiner Settled on the Guadalupe

Charles Schreiner, born in Alsace-Lorraine, February 22, 1838, came to San Antonio in 1852. After ranger service Schreiner and his brother-in-law, Casper Real, moved to Turtle Creek and began ranching in 1857. Kerr County had been organized the year before. Schreiner sold wood, hay, and cattle to the Army at Camp Verde. He served three and a half years in the Confederate Army.

In 1869, when Kerrville had 200 residents—and the nearest stores were in Comfort and Fredericksburg — Schreiner borrowed $5,000 from August Faltin, of Comfort, to buy merchandise and build a small cypress shack. From sales of $3.50—7½ pounds of coffee, $2, and two quarts of whiskey, $1.50—on his first day, Christmas Eve, Schreiner's business prospered. Since there was little cash in the country, receipts were mainly in shingles, lumber, bear grease, honey and hides. Schreiner recalled:

> The first year we had no safe. There was a loose board in the floor of the store. Our vault had no time lock. When darkness came I simply raised the loose board, deposited the accumulated coins under the floor, replaced the board, and rolled a barrel over it. The first year our sales, all told, amounted to about $5,000.
>
> When cattle were bought they were paid for in gold or silver. From the very first we did banking business. The cattle buyers would bring Spanish doubloons —a gold coin of about the equivalent of sixteen dollars—and silver dollars in morrals hung on their saddle horns. They would turn the money over to us for safe keeping and give orders on us for payment for cattle.

Schreiner's was mainly a credit business. After selling cattle or wool the customer would pay on his account. J. Evetts Haley noted in his fine book that Dave Wharton, who charged his purchase the day the store opened, kept an open account for the rest of his life and had an outstanding balance when he died.

Casper Real brought the first sheep into the country. Schreiner encouraged sheepraising, sometimes making loans to ranchers contingent upon their going into the sheep business. By 1889 his banking business had become so extensive that the Charles Schreiner Bank was established. His 500,000 acre ranch extended to Menard, eighty miles away. Schreiner was also the Kerr County treasurer from 1869 to 1898.

One of those who worked for Schreiner was Simon Ayala, who carried gold in a horse's nose bag to San Antonio for banking. (Ayala broke horses using a trough built into one stirrup to accomodate his wooden leg and sometimes whacking obstreperous animals on the head with the artificial limb.) Nathan Herzog, a German-born Jew, clerked at the store from 1874 until after Charles Schreiner's death in 1927. A small man, he could carry a 200-pound sack of stock salt out to a customer or load a 350-pound barrel of sugar into a wagon by himself, yet women trusted him to pick out hats for them.

When Schreiner endowed Schreiner Institute, which opened in 1923, his gift of $550,000 was then the largest ever made to a denominational college in the South.

Charles Schreiner's practice of holding customers' funds for them grew into Kerrville's Schreiner Bank.

Ormsby Rode the Butterfield Overland Mail

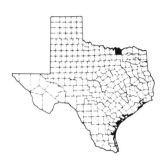

The Butterfield Overland Mail grew out of the need to connect California with the rest of the nation. John Butterfield—who controlled several stage lines and was a founder of American Express—and his associates agreed, in September, 1857, to furnish semi-weekly mail service between the Mississippi River and San Francisco for $600,000 a year. Service was to begin within a year; preparations included the improvement of old roads and opening of new ones over a 2800-mile route, hiring personnel, establishing stations, and buying a thousand horses, five hundred mules, and one hundred coaches and wagons.

By the time the first runs were made, 141 stations were ready; some sixty more were opened later. The home stations would serve meals and make repairs. The swing stations were only for changing teams. The coach was manned by a driver, who covered about sixty miles, and a conductor, who rode 120 miles. The conductor was in charge of the coach, mail, and passengers; his duties included warning stations of their approach by bugle call so that the teams might be changed quickly. Service was begun just prior to the deadline. An eastbound stage left San Francisco as another headed west from St. Louis, a third stage, from Memphis, joined the westbound at Fort Smith. The eastbound fare was $100, and westbound passengers paid $200.

Waterman Ormsby, a twenty-three-year-old reporter for the *New York Herald*, was the sole passenger on the initial California run, which took nearly 24 days. Until then 40 days was required for a letter to come from California. From St. Louis Ormsby traveled by rail 160 miles to Tipton, Missouri, and by stagecoach to Springfield; from there to San Francisco Ormsby rode in canvas-topped wagons which had leather straps instead of springs. The three seats inside had backs which folded down to "form one bed capable of accomodating from four to ten persons, according to size and how they lie."

The route entered Texas in Grayson County; the Chickasaw Nation had authorized Benjamin Colbert to operate a ferry across Red River. Ormsby wrote:

> Mr. Colbert, the owner of the station and of the ferry is a half-breed Indian of great sagacity and business tact. He is a young man—not quite thirty, I should judge—and has a white wife—his third.

Colbert ferried the stage without charge because of the business the mail service would generate. His large raft was poled across the Red River by slaves.

At Sherman, which Ormsby called a pleasant little village of about six hundred, the team was ready, but at Diamond's station, he witnessed the harnessing of a wild mule:

> First he had to be secured with a larette around his neck, and drawn by main force to a tree or post; then the harness had to be put on piece by piece, care being taken to avoid his teeth and heels. Altogether I should estimate the time consumed in the process at not less than half an hour to each wild mule, and that, when the mail has to wait for it, I think, might much better be spent on the road . . . . no doubt when all the company's wild mules are tamed the mail will make better time.

At Gainesville, thirteen miles away, supper was served. Good time was made over the fifteen miles to Davidson's station where "there was nothing in readiness."

90

Citizens marked the route of the Butterfield Overland Mail through Sherman.

The month-old road from Sherman to Belknap was already well-marked by wagons. At Conolly's station Ormsby had breakfast in the one-room, mud-chinked log house:

> ... served on the bottom of a candle box, and such as sat down were perched on inverted pails or nature's chair. There were not plates enough and but four tin cups for the coffee, which was served without milk or sugar. As there were six of us, including drivers and workmen, those not lucky enough to get a first cup had to wait for the second table. The edible—for there was but one—consisted of a kind of shortcake, baked on the coals, each man breaking off his chunk and plastering on butter with his pocket knife; but butter is a rare luxury between the Red River and the Rio Grande . . . .

Earhart's station was 20 miles away. The next stop was Jacksboro, one year old but with a population of 200.

> It is on the edge of a large plain which, as we approached it, looked like a passive lake, so even and level was its surface . . . . Our mules were exceedingly stubborn and lazy during the night and required the most constant urging to keep them on a respectable trot. It would seem to me that horses might be employed with both economy of time and labor . . . .

They reached Fort Belknap, on the Brazos in Young County, on September 22. Two companies of cavalry were stationed there, and a town with a "billiard saloon" and post office had developed. The Brazos was low, "not deeper than an ordinary New York gutter." At the Clear Fork station the Brazos was not so clear, but Ormsby bathed in its waters anyway; the team was changed so quickly he had to finish dressing in the wagon. The crew at Smith's station was living in tents while building the facilities. "They had nearly finished a fine corral for the stock, making it of brush (for no timber could be had) and filling in the chinks with mud." Ormsby was grateful for a woman's cooking, although the fare was about the same, "cake cooked in the coals, clear coffee, and some dried beef cooked in Mrs. Smith's best style."

At Phantom Hill, 74 miles from Fort Belknap, Ormsby saw the ruins of half a million dollars worth of government property burned by departing soldiers.

> It was said that the officers and men were heartily disgusted with the station and wished to make certain of never going back; that, as they were leaving the fort, one of the principal officers was heard to say that he wished the place would burn down; and that the soldiers, taking him at his word, stayed behind and fired the buildings.

The Butterfield company was using the least damaged buildings, making it the best of the new stations.

> Mr. Burlington and his wife we found here all alone, hundreds of miles from any settlement, bravely standing their post on Phantom Hill, fearless of the attacks of bloodthirsty Indians—as brave a man as ever settled on a frontier and a monument of shame to the cowardly soldiers who burned the post . . . . The station is directly in the trail of the northern Comanches as they run down into Texas on their marauding expeditions.

There were no mules at Phantom Hill, so the team, which had already covered 34 miles, could not be changed before Abercrombie Pass, 15 miles away; there the meal was served by an aged Negro woman who "if cleanliness is next to Godliness, would stand little chance of heaven. There is an old saying 'every man must eat his peck of dirt.' I think I have had good measure with my peck on this trip . . . ."

At Fort Chadbourne, on the Little Colorado River, Ormsby complained of the delay in changing teams:

> Whether from the inefficiency of Mr. Nichols' driving, or because Mr. Mather's furious riding frightened the mules, or because the mules were wild, or that the boys had been having a jolly good time on the occasion of the arrival of the first stage, or by a special dispensation of Providence—or from a combination of all these causes—I will not pretend to say, but certainly from some unforeseen and vexatious cause we here suffered a detention of some hours. The mules reared, pitched, twisted, whirled, wheeled, ran, stood still, and cut up all sorts of capers. The wagon performed so many evolutions that I, in fear of my life, abandoned it and took to my heels, fully confident that I could make more progress in a straight line, with much less risk of breaking my neck.

Ormsby was glad he dismounted:

> ... for the gyrations continued to considerable length, winding up with tangling all the mules pretty well in the harness, the escape of one of the leaders into the woods, and the complete demolition of the top of the wagon; while those in charge of it lay around loose on the grass, and all were pretty tired and disgusted except those who had nothing to do but look on.

The lead mules gone, the driver intended to proceed with only two mules. Ormsby got back into the wagon, "though if I had had any property I certainly should have made a hasty will."

At the Grape Creek station they got a full team, and since it was so far to the next stop they took along four extra mules. On September 25—55 miles west of Fort Chadbourne—they reached the edge of the Staked Plains.

> The low rate of speed between Chadbourne and El Paso is accounted for by the fact that the route comprises an entirely wild country across the great Staked Plain, 75 miles without water, and 113 up the sierras, where stations had not been established. In fact, there is not a human habitation, except the company stations, on the whole distance of over 400 miles.

At Hueco Tanks they found very little water. Fort Bliss, two miles from Franklin—present El Paso—had a small garrison living in adobe buildings. Ormsby did not cross the Rio Grande to the Mexican city of El Paso, present Juarez. At Franklin, to Ormsby's gratification, the mules were exchanged for horses. They were to meet the eastbound stage there, since Franklin was the halfway point—1,308 miles from St. Louis and 1,332 from San Francisco—but the meeting actually took place a hundred miles to the west. From Franklin to California the country was uninhabited except for such villages as Tucson and Fort Yuma. The route swung down into Mexico just before turning north to Los Angeles and San Francisco.

The greatest immediate contribution of the Butterfield Overland Mail was in transmitting news, which could be sent by wire from the telegraph terminus, thus reducing the time by a week. In 1860 the Pony Express destroyed this news-carrying advantage. As secession approached it became impossible to operate the stages through Texas, and the Butterfield line's last eastbound mail left California in early April, 1861.

John Reagan Was the Old Roman

Tennessee-born John Henninger Reagan came to Texas in 1839 when he was twenty years old. He took part in the Cherokee war and most of the other events that shaped nineteenth-century Texas. The offices he held included justice of the peace, county judge, militia colonel, district judge, congressman, United States Senator, Railroad Commissioner, and Confederate Postmaster General.

Reagan settled near present Alto, Cherokee County, and surveyed in the territory to the west, where he almost died in a norther; hours after Reagan lost consciousness from the cold his horse stopped at King's Fort, in present Kaufman County; Rip Ford and others immersed him, fully-dressed, in cold water, then gradually warmed the room. When Reagan revived he was put to bed; although his skin looked scalded, he survived.

In 1842 he became a Nacogdoches County justice of the peace and captain of militia. He farmed for awhile in present Kaufman County, read law, and began practice in 1846 at Buffalo, the capital of Henderson County; he was the first county judge and was elected to the legislature. Athens having become the Henderson County seat, Reagan moved to Palestine; he became the district judge in 1852.

Reagan was a congressman at the time of the John Brown raid. After Lincoln's election, Reagan and others began planning a secession convention. Reagan was one of seven Texans sent to Montgomery, Alabama, as delegates to the new government and was a Confederate congressman when President Jefferson Davis made him Postmaster General. He and Davis were captured in Georgia by Union troops in May, 1865. Reagan was imprisoned at Fort Warren, near Boston, for 22 weeks and returned to Texas on military parole near the close of 1865. Finding Texans critical of a letter he had written from prison advising cooperation with the Federals, Reagan retired to his neglected farm at Palestine.

In 1874, after the end of Governor Davis' radical Republican administration, Reagan was elected to Congress; he served in the state constitutional convention before taking his congressional seat. Reagan's most important work in Washington concerned railroad regulation and resulted in establishment of the Interstate Commerce Commission.

Governor James Hogg persuaded Reagan to leave the Senate and become chairman of the new Texas Railroad Commission in 1891. Although too old for such strenuous service, Reagan was guided by duty, something he had done often enough to be called "the old Roman." When he retired, in 1903, the new regulatory body was on solid ground. Back at Palestine, he wrote his memoirs and pondered six decades of public service. He ventured horseback into another norther, contracted pneumonia, and died March 6, 1905.

Old Fort Houston was located on land which became a part of John Reagan's Palestine farm.

Dick Dowling Turned Back a Yankee Army

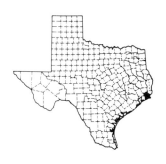

The most spectacular Confederate victory—which Jefferson Davis called the "Thermopylae of the Civil War"—occurred at Sabine Pass. There Lt. Richard Dowling and 46 others captured some 400 sailors and soldiers and turned back an invasion force of at least 4,000 troops without sustaining a single casualty.

Born in July, 1838, Dowling came to New Orleans from Ireland as a boy. After his parents died of yellow fever, he moved to Texas, married, and was living in Houston when the war began. He was commissioned in Captain Frederick Odlum's Davis Guards, a company of Irish stevedores, section hands, and laborers.

Confederate Major General John B. Magruder knew of the Federals' intention to invade Texas and halt shipment of cotton into Mexico to be exchanged for guns and ammunition. The Confederates were able to assign only a small force to Sabine Pass; about five miles above the mouth of the pass the Davis Guards were completing Fort Griffin, an earthwork fortification with the embankments on three sides strengthened by timbers. Four of its six guns had been discarded by the United States Army. As General Banks' invasion fleet lay off Sabine Pass, Magruder ordered the fort destroyed and its men withdrawn, but Captain Odlum left the decision to Lt. Dowling, the commander of the fort. Dowling chose to fight.

Sabine Pass had a narrow entrance and was bordered by mud flats. About a mile below Fort Griffin the Sabine widened considerably because of an oyster reef, three hundred yards wide, in the middle; this created a channel on either side. Fort Griffin extended slightly into the western, or Texas, channel. Its guns commanded both channels. If federal forces could get past the fort they could land troops and capture it with ease. A successful invasion of Sabine Pass would give the Federals control of the coast, and the interiors of Texas and Louisiana could be invaded at leisure.

The Federals decided to land troops on the only dry land below Fort Griffin. On September 8, 1863, the gunboats *Sachem* and *Arizona* would proceed up the eastern, or Louisiana, channel and engage the fort in an artillery duel. While the Confederates were so occupied two gunboats, with army sharpshooters aboard, would lead the transports up the Texas channel and provide covering fire while the troops were put ashore. Lt. Dowling made the following report of the action:

> On Monday morning, about two o'clock the sentinel informed me that the enemy were signalling, and fearing an attack I ordered all the guns at the fort manned and remained in that position until daylight, at which time there were two steamers evidently sounding for the channel on the bar; a large frigate outside. They remained all day at work, but during the evening were re-enforced to the number of twenty-two vessels of different classes.
>
> On the morning of the 8th, the U.S. gunboat *Clifton* anchored opposite the lighthouse and fired twenty-six shells at the fort, most of which passed a little over or fell short; all, however, in excellent range, one shell being landed on the works and another striking the south angle of the fort, without doing any material damage. The firing commenced at 6:30 o'clock and finished at 7:30 o'clock by the gunboat hauling off. During this time we had not replied by a single shot . . . . The whole fleet then drew off and remained out of range until 3:40 o'clock, when the *Sachem* and the *Arizona* steamed into line up the Louisiana channel, the *Clifton* and one boat, name unknown, remaining at the junction of the two channels. I allowed the two former boats to approach within 1,200

Dick Dowling and a handful of Irishmen turned back a Federal invasion at Sabine Pass.

yards when I opened fire with the whole of my battery on the foremost boat (the *Sachem*) which, after the third or fourth round, hoisted the white flag, one of the shots passing through her steam drum. The *Clifton*, in the meantime, had attempted to pass through the Texas channel, but receiving a shot which carried away her tiller rope, she became unmanageable and grounded about 500 yards below the fort, which enabled me to concentrate all my guns on her, which were six in number—two 32-pounder smooth bores, two 24-pounder smooth bores, two 32-pounder howitzers. She withstood our fire some twenty-five or thirty minutes, when she also hoisted a white flag. During the time she was aground, she used grape, and her sharpshooters poured an incessant shower of Minie balls into the works. The fight lasted from the time I fired the first gun until the boats surrendered; that was about three-quarters of an hour. .

After mentioning four officers who were at Fort Griffin with his 42 Irishmen during the engagement, Dowling wrote, "Thus it will be seen that we captured with 47 men two gunboats mounting thirteen guns of the heaviest caliber and about 350 prisoners."

With the channels blocked by the disabled gunboats, the invasion force withdrew. Colonel Duganne, a prisoner of war at Camp Groce, 75 miles away, was bitterly disappointed. He wrote:

The American squadron and army . . . had retreated from the coast . . . shamefully driven off by 42 Irish militiamen in a mud fort with six pieces of artillery! The details, as I have said, we learned through the recital of prisoners like ourselves . . . skirmishers in front of the Yankee army of six thousand men, in 26 transports, hugging the Sabine Bar, these new prisoners—some 400 in number—arrived a few days afterward to tell us the story of Sabine Pass. . . .

The gunboat *Sachem* had been disabled by a Confederate shot which struck its boiler, and killed thirty crewmen. Then, the *Clifton* grounded on a sandbar. Of these two gunboats, Duganne complained:

. . . the enemy boarded them in spite of our army and its generals. Three hundred gallant soldiers and sailors were suffered to be carried away prisoners without a shot being fired in an effort to rescue them.

The Confederate Congress passed a commendation resolution which described the invasion force as five gunboats and 22 transports with 25,000 men. The participants were given medals. The *Clifton* was repaired by the Confederates and used for a few months before it ran aground. The *Sachem* became a Confederate blockade runner and was sold with her cargo at Vera Cruz. After the war Dick Dowling operated his saloon at Main and Congress in Houston. He died of yellow fever in 1867 at the age of 29 years and was buried at St. Vincent's Cemetery.

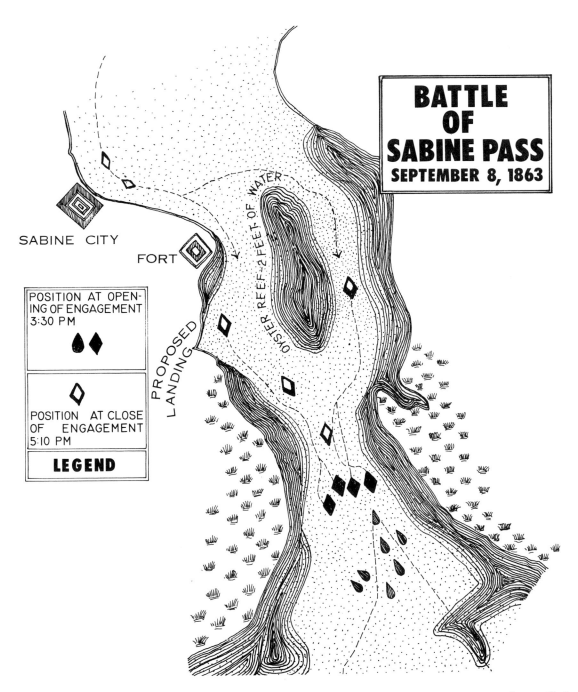

BATTLE OF SABINE PASS
SEPTEMBER 8, 1863

SABINE CITY

FORT

OYSTER REEF-2 FEET OF WATER

PROPOSED LANDING

POSITION AT OPEN-
ING OF ENGAGEMENT
3:30 PM

POSITION AT CLOSE
OF ENGAGEMENT
5:10 PM

LEGEND

—Lynn Guier

Dick Dowling's fort commanded both Texas and Louisiana channels, left and right above. The Federals hoped gunboats in the Louisiana channel would keep Dowling's guns occupied while another gunboat led transports up the Texas channel and unloaded troops on the only dry land below the fort. The plan failed as Dowling's guns disabled the gunboats, blocking both channels.

James Throckmorton Was an Impediment to Reconstruction

James Webb Throckmorton, born February 1, 1825, on the Calf Killer River near Sparta, Tennessee, came to Texas when he was sixteen. After stopping at Warren, Fannin County, his father, Dr. William Throckmorton, settled the family near present Melissa in early 1842. Dr. Throckmorton, who is considered to be the first Collin County settler, died in October, 1843; Throckmorton County was named for him. After doing some ranger duty, in 1844 James Throckmorton began the study of medicine under his uncle, Dr. James. E. Throckmorton, at Princeton, Kentucky. He returned to Texas when the Mexican War began and joined Captain Robert H. Taylor's company as a private. In Mexico he was made second surgeon in Walter P. Lane's battalion but became ill and received a medical discharge in June, 1847.

Throckmorton married Annie Rattan in February, 1848, and they had ten children. He was practicing medicine near McKinney but was not happy. He wrote his cousin, "I had studied medicine to gratify your grandfather. The profession was exceedingly distasteful to me, but an unrelenting necessity forced me to follow it." He began studying law in 1849 and was elected, as a Democrat, to the legislature in 1851. He was re-elected twice, then entered the Texas Senate. As the slavery controversy intensified Throckmorton's opposition to secession grew. In 1859 he deserted the Democratic candidate, Hardin Runnels, to support the Unionist, Sam Houston, for the governorship.

Some Southerners considered Lincoln's election the test of whether the Union should be maintained. Eighteen free states gave Abraham Lincoln 1,857,610 popular and 180 electoral ballots. Democrat Stephen Douglas had 1,365,976 popular votes and twelve electors. Former vice president Breckenridge's 847,953 popular, and 72 electoral, votes came from eleven slave states, and Unionist John Bell received 590,631 ballots and 39 electors from Kentucky, Tennessee, and Virginia. Breckenridge, the Southern Democrat, carried Texas; the canvass reflected no votes in the state for either Lincoln or Douglas.

South Carolina seceded on December 20, 1860. Sentiment for immediate disunion was strong in Texas. Ignoring Governor Sam Houston, secession leaders called a convention for January 28, 1861, at Austin. Each representative district was to elect two delegates; as a candidate Throckmorton argued that the southern states could best serve their interests by remaining in the Union. In spite of being on the unpopular side of the issue, Throckmorton was elected. He was against secession, but he also believed the coercion of a state might justify disunion.

On January 28, the 177 delegates elected Oran M. Roberts president. As the convention met in the House chamber on February 1 to vote on the secession ordinance Governor Houston, hoping to avoid disunion, was present. Only delegates Hughes, of Williamson County, Johnson, of Titus County, Johnson, of Lamar County, and Shuford, of Wood County, had cast negative votes when Throckmorton said, "In view of the responsibility, in the presence of God and my country—and unawed by the wild spirit of revolution around me, I vote no." When a spectator voiced disapproval, Throckmorton rose again and added, "Mr. President, when the rabble hiss, well may patriots tremble."

The secession ordinance was passed 167 to seven, with L. H. Williams and George W. Wright joining the other dissenters. If Texas were to remain in the Union, secession had to be defeated at the polls on February 23. In referring the question to the

Collin County erected a statue to the memory of Governor James Throckmorton, the son of the county's first settler.

people, the convention cited the offenses of the northern states and warned that Texas had to follow the six seceded states or be isolated.

Throckmorton was sufficiently persuasive to keep Collin County from supporting the ordinance, and some other north Texas counties voted against secession, but statewide results were 44,129 to 14,697 for separation. Throckmorton told the convention:

> I believe we are on the verge of a long, bloody war, the consequences of which none can forsee. While my judgment dictates to me that we are not justified by the surroundings or the occasion, a majority of the people of Texas have declared in favor of secession . . . the time will soon be upon us when the clash of arms will be heard . . . when it comes I will be in its midst . . . .

He swore to support the Confederacy. Continued opposition would encourage civil strife; furthermore, the Federal government had no right to coerce the states. Throckmorton served in the Indian Territory, Arkansas, and Mississippi with state and Confederate troops. After his election to the Texas Senate, he urged support of the war effort, for defeat would mean: "You and your sons will become renters of your own soil and wanderers on the face of the earth." In 1864 he became a brigadier general of state troops. He was also an Indian commissioner charged with making treaties with the tribes north of Red River.

After the Confederate collapse Governor Pendleton Murrah fled to Mexico. President Andrew Johnson appointed A. J. Hamilton provisional governor on June 17, 1865. In the next year Throckmorton defeated E. M. Pease for the governorship. As governor he was exasperated by the army's unwillingness to move its soldiers to the frontier instead of keeping them in the interior to guard against disloyalty. The military chose to believe the Indian raids were not as bad as represented. Throckmorton's relations with General Philip Sheridan were bad from the beginning. After Congressional Reconstruction was implemented on March 2, 1867, Texas was part of the fifth military district and her civil officers were provisional only. Eleven days after a supplementary act gave him power to depose state officials Sheridan declared:

> . . . J. W. Throckmorton, Governor of Texas, is an impediment to the reconstruction of that state under the law; he is therefore removed . . . .

After serving exactly one year, on August 8, 1867, Throckmorton turned over the governorship to E. M. Pease. Having to sell his gold watch to meet expenses, he wrote, "My sojourn at Austin left me $1200 worse off than it found me, notwithstanding my economy." Governor Pease eventually became fed up with the military and resigned.

Later, Throckmorton served several terms in Congress. He was tendered the post of Secretary of the Interior in Grover Cleveland's second administration, but his health would not permit him to serve. He was stricken while in court at McKinney and died on April 21, 1894.

Governor James W. Throckmorton was removed from office by General Philip Sheridan.

Peter Robinson Bought a Place in Meridian

When Mrs. Mariah Robinson sat for an interview during the depression she was well past ninety. Born a slave, she had midwifed hundreds of Bosque County babies, black and white. Ten of her own eleven children reached maturity. Her lifetime had spanned the war with Mexico, the Civil War, Indian troubles, the Spanish-American War, World War I, and the great depression. Her husband had died at age 86, and she assumed she was near the close of her own life. But she was wrong; she lived through World War II and died September 25, 1946, at approximately 108 years of age. This is what she told the interviewer:

I's borned over in Georgia, in that place call Monroe, and Mammy was Lizzie Hill, 'cause her massa Judge Hill. I's honest, I don't know the 'zact date I's borned. Missy Jo, my missy, put the record of all ages in the courthouse for safekeeping, to keep the Indians from burning them up, and they's burnt up when the courthouse burns. All I knows is my youngest sister, what live in Georgia, writ me 'bout a year ago and say, "Last Thursday I's 81 year old." There is five children 'twixt my and her age, and there is six children younger'n me. That the best I can give of my age.

Judge Hill's daughter, Miss Josephine, married Dr. Young's son what lived in Cartersville, in Georgia, but had done moved to Texas. Then my missy give me to Miss Josephine to come to Texas with her to keep her from the lonely hours and being sad so far 'way from home. We come by rail from Monroe to Social Circle and there boards the boat "Sweet Home." There was just two boats on the line, the "Sweet Home" and the "Katie Darling."

Us sails down the Atlantic Ocean to New Orleans, myself and my Aunt Lonnie and Uncle Johns, all with Miss Josephine . . . . Coming down the Mississippi 'cross the Gulf, us seed no land for days and days, and us go through the Gulf of Mexico and lands at the port, Galveston, and us come to Waco on the stagecoach.

Us live four year on Austin Street in Waco, that four year 'fore the war of 1861. Us boarded with Dr. Tinsley, and he and General Ross was good friends. I worked in a sewing-room, doing work such as whipping on laces and ruffling and tucking. Then us come to Bosque County right near Meridian 'cause Massa Bob have the ranch there, and the time of the Freedom War us lives there.

Us be in the house at night, peeping out the window or pigeonhole and see Indians coming. The chief lead in front. They wild Comanches. Sometime there fifty or sixty in a bunch, and they did raiding at night. But I's pretty brave and goes three mile to Walnut Spring every day to get vegetables. I rid the donkey. Miss Josephine boards all the Bosque County school children, and us have to git the food. I seed droves of wild turkey and buffaloes and antelopes and deers. I seed wildcats and coons and bunches of wolves and heared the panther scream like the woman.

Us lived in a log cabin with two chimneys and a long shedroom and cooked in the kitchen fireplace in the skillet and over the pot racks. Us made meal on the steel mill and hominy and cheese. I got the prize for spinning and weaving. I knitted the stockins, but Miss Jo had to drap the stitch for me to turn the heels and toes.

During the Freedom War Massa General Bob Young git kilt at the last battle. That the Bull Run battle, and he fit under General Lee. That left my missy the war widow, and she mammy come live with her and she teached in the school. I stays with them four year after freedom, and I's one of the family

After Mariah Robinson insisted upon a home, her husband built a house on this land at Meridian.

for the board and the clothes. They's good to me and likes to make me the best-looking and neatest slave in that place. I had such as pretty starched dresses, and they holp me fix the hair nice.

Us used the soft, dim candlelight, and I make the candlesticks. Us have gourd dippers and oak buckets to dip water out the well, and us make wooden tubs out of stumps and battling sticks to clean the clothes.

I done already met up with Peter Robinson. He's the slave of Massa Ridley Robinson what was gwine to California from Alabama, with all he slaves. Massa Robinson git kilt by the Mexicans, and a white man name Gibb Smith gits to own Peter. He hires him out to a farmer clost by us ranch, and I gits to meet him, and us have the courtship and gits married. That 'fore freedom. Us married by Caesar Berry, the slave of Massa Buck Berry. Caesar am the colored preacher. Pete was 'telligent and 'liable and the good man. He played the fiddle all over the country, and I rid horseback with him miles and miles to them dances.

Peter could write the plain hand, and he gits to haul lumber from Waco to make the Bosque County courthouse. He larns more and gits to be the county's first colored trustee and the first colored teacher. He gits 'pinted to see after the widows in time of war and in the 'construction days. Finally, he is sont to Austin, the capital of Texas, to be representative.

Pete and me begot ten children. My first child am borned two months 'fore freedom. After us slaves is freed, us hired out for one year to get means to go free on. Us held by the committee call "Free Committee Men." The wages is ten dollars the month to the family. After us ready to go for ourselves, my missy am the poor widow, and she have only three cows and three calves, but she give one of each of them to Pete and me.

After leaving Miss Jo, us move here and yonder till I gits tired of such. By then us have several children, and I changes from the frivolity of life to the sincereness, to shape the destiny of the children's life. I tells Pete, when he comes back from fiddling one night, to buy me the home or hitch up and carry me back to Missy Jo. That lead him to buy a strip of land in Meridian. He pay ten dollar the acre. We has a team of oxen, call Broad and Buck, and we done our farming with them. Pete builds me a house, hauls the lumber from Waco. Twicet us gits burnt out, but builds it 'gain. Us makes the orchard and sells the fruit. Us raises bees and sells the honey and gits cows and chickens and turkeys. Pete works good, and I puts on my bonnet and walks behind him and draps the corn.

He gits in organizing the first colored church in Meridian, the colored Cumberland Presbyterian Church. Us has ever lived the useful life. I works at cooking and washing and ironing. I helps the doctors with the babies.

But the disability of age have to come, and now I is 'most disabled and feels stunted and poverty-stricken. I'd like to work now, but I isn't able.

Mariah Robinson and daughter, Lula.   —*Ella Robinson*
Mariah Robinson at 104 years of age.
Peter Robinson and sons.

A Fort Was Established on the Conchos

The first settlers reached the Concho River country in 1864. Soon after the close of the Civil War a commission planning a line of defense on the Texas frontier decided one fort should be built at the junction of the North and South Concho rivers. The officer sent to establish the post disapproved of the location and built Fort Concho on its present site, for which he was dismissed from the Army. Speculators bought the necessary land and leased it to the United States for $100 a year with the understanding that the buildings would belong to the landowners upon abandonment of the fort.

Camp Hatch, named for Major John P. Hatch, was founded in December, 1867, with a garrison of five cavalry companies; in February it was renamed Fort Concho. Construction was difficult and costly because of the scarcity of materials. The first buildings, all of sandstone, were finished by March 1870; they included a commissary, quartermaster's storehouses, a hospital, a magazine, five officers' quarters, and two barracks. The facilities would accomodate six cavalry troops and two infantry companies. Within the decade the fort grew to 39 buildings and stables, reflecting its importance in that new country.

Fredericksburg, the nearest town, was 150 miles away, and supplies had to come 225 miles from San Antonio. Buffalo roamed the post, especially in dry seasons. There were antelope, deer, and wolves in abundance, and 75-pound catfish were caught in the Concho rivers. Seven-inch centipedes were reported, as well as three-inch scorpions. Three miles away was Ben Ficklin's stage stop, where a few people had settled; across the North Concho a saloon and some stores were opened to relieve the soldiers of their pay, which was $13 a month for privates. This sod-house, dugout, and shanty community of three dozen inhabitants, "Over the River," became San Angelo in the early seventies.

Among the commanders of Fort Concho were: William R. Shafter, a Civil War brigadier general and winner of the Congressional Medal of Honor, who led campaigns against the Comanche, explored the new country west of Fort Concho, and, as a major general, commanded the American troops in Cuba during the Spanish-American War; Benjamin H. Grierson, a music teacher who became a major general of cavalry during the Civil War after leading several spectacular raids, and who commanded the 10th Cavalry of black soldiers from 1866 to 1890; and Ranald Slidell Mackenzie. General Grant said, "I regarded Mackenzie as the most promising young officer in the Army." Mackenzie was the best of the Indian fighters. One of his men wrote, "Mackenzie hung on like a bulldog until the Indians begged him to let go. He dealt the heavy blows which finally forced the Comanche onto the reservation at Fort Sill." Later he was a brigadier general commanding the Department of Texas.

Among the units stationed at Fort Concho were the 9th and 10th Cavalry regiments, black troops called "Buffalo Soldiers" by the plains Indians; the men took such pride in the name that the emblem adopted by Grierson's 10th Cavalry was a shield surmounted by a buffalo. Grierson said of them, "Colored troops will hold their place in the Army of the United States as long as the government lasts."

The main building of San Angelo's Fort Concho is now a museum.

From 1878 to 1881 Fort Concho was headquarters of the District of the Pecos. Grierson supervised forts Davis, Stockton, Griffin, and eight smaller posts while commanding Fort Concho.

Fort Griffin was abandoned in 1881 and there was some question about the need for Fort Concho. The railroad from Ballinger reached San Angelo in 1888, and a few months later the last company at Fort Concho was transferred. The troops paraded out of the fort and into San Angelo on June 20, 1889, and all the equipment was shipped to San Antonio. The men buried at Fort Concho were moved to a San Antonio military cemetery.

This trooper, a member of the Ninth Cavalry, was stationed at Fort Concho.

Fort Richardson Was on the Edge of Civilization

After the Confederacy fell it was necessary that a line of forts be established for the protection of settlers in the frontier counties. The post proposed for Jacksboro was the northernmost; the Indian Territory was only seventy miles away. Part of the Sixth Cavalry, commanded by Colonel S. H. Starr, moved into Jacksboro on July 4, 1866, and pitched tents on the square. The town consisted of a few stone, concrete, and frame structures used for business and government and scattered log houses, remnants of a thriving pre-war community.

H. H. McConnell, a man of perception and wit, left an invaluable account of Fort Richardson and Jacksboro. Writing of their isolation, he noted:

> Toward the west, with the exception of two or three families in Young County, no settlement existed between Jacksboro and the Rio Grande; northward an unbroken wilderness stretched to the Kansas line; to the northwest an occasional Mexican settlement in northern New Mexico only interrupted the route to Santa Fe . . . .

In early 1867 the Tonkawa guides and scouts arrived. Friendly toward the whites and once much more numerous, the Tonkawa were fewer than 200. While the troops at Jacksboro were still living in tents, the War Department assigned two companies to Buffalo Springs and the other four companies to old Fort Belknap in Young County. Belknap had been abandoned when General Twiggs surrendered all Federal property in 1861. Only three or four soldiers remained at Jacksboro to carry the mail to and from Weatherford.

The camp at Buffalo Springs, 25 miles from Jacksboro, was the only human habitation in Clay County. Civilians accompanied the troops to build a fort there. After a large party raided Wise County in July, 1867, Fort Sill was established on Cache Creek in the Indian Territory a hundred miles north of Jacksboro. Because the Buffalo Springs site proved to be an unfortunate choice, that November a permanent post was located on Jacksboro's Lost Creek and named for General Israel Richardson, who died at Antietam in 1862.

About 150 civilians, paid $3 to $5 a day, came to build Fort Richardson; they were assisted by soldiers who earned an extra 40¢ a day. Thus half a million dollars in federal funds were pumped into the local economy annually between 1868 and 1873, making Jacksboro a boomtown. McConnell said it blossomed "if not 'like the rose,' at least like a sunflower, and gorgeous and euphonious names graced the board or picket shanties that dotted the hillside and invited the thirsty and unwary to enter. There was the 'Union Headquarters,' . . . the 'Gem,' the 'Little Shamrock,' . . . the 'First National,' the 'Last Chance,' and the sound of the fiddle and the crack of the six-shooter was heard the livelong night."

Fort Richardson was well-planned. The hospital, commissary, bakery, and guardhouse were good stone buildings. McConnell wrote of the hospital:

> At many posts, if not at the majority of them, the hospital is so inhospitable as to present few attractions, and all keep away from it as long as possible, the prospect promising less comfort than the barracks . . . but Fort Richardson being intended for a first-class post, the hospital was speedily finished, and was a fine brick building with two large wards, each with a capacity of twelve beds, a maximum of air space, broad verandas, fine ventilation, and every accessory necessary to the comforts of the inmates.

Fort Richardson's hospital at Jacksboro has been turned into a museum.

The presence of Fort Richardson stimulated commercial activity, including the building of a new Jack County courthouse and an increase in traffic. McConnell enjoyed the stagecoach drivers, whose colorful personalities were shaped by having to cope with the wild mules.

> It was fun to see the stage start for Fort Concho in those days; the driver would mount the box and gather up his lines, Eastburn (the agent) and his clerks each holding a mule by the head; then at a signal they would let go—and off went the team like the wind. The driver, after a spin around the block for a mile or two, would get back to the postoffice, load up the immense mail, and pull out on a dead run.

Because most federal soldiers were on occupation duty in the interior, the frontier posts were lightly manned. Only two companies were at Fort Richardson in the summer of 1869, and little attention was paid to Indian defense since most of the soldiers were doing construction work and other duty incident to running the post. McConnell, then a Fort Richardson sergeant, was amazed by the indifference of the government to conditions in West Texas:

> The fact that this is a frontier does not seem to be known to the authorities at Washington or elsewhere. In 1867, when the blazing dwellings of the pioneers of Texas lighted up the sky from the Red River to the Rio Grande, when desolated homes, murdered women and captured children were every-day occurrences along our whole frontier, General Sheridan in a report stated that "no Indian difficulties of any importance had occurred in his department; that the Red River was a sort of dead-line over which neither Indian nor Texan dared to cross owing to the hostility of one to the other;" . . . this, too, at a time when the garrison at Buffalo Springs was beseiged for days by five hundred Indians, and when appeal after appeal had been sent to General Sheridan for arms and ammunition.

Frontier neglect continued until the Salt Creek Massacre occurred in 1871 while General of the Army William T. Sherman was visiting Fort Richardson.

In April, 1871, Colonel Ranald Mackenzie's Fourth Cavalry relieved the Sixth Cavalry at Fort Richardson, a change which McConnell considered a blessing; he had great respect for Mackenzie.

> He was a fighting man, had achieved a national reputation during the war, was one of the youngest Generals in the volunteer service and the youngest Colonel in the regular army. He believed it was more important for the troops to scout the frontier and perform military duty than it was to build chicken-coops for officers and interfere with the citizens of the country; and within two years after he took command, the occupation of the Indian was gone, the lives of the settlers were safe, and the early abandonment of numerous military stations possible, they being no longer needed.

A few troops remained at Richardson until the spring of 1878, when the post was abandoned and the buildings were taken over by the landowner.

The Fort Richardson morgue was occupied by Satanta and Big Tree while awaiting trial in Jacksboro.

Satanta Was Tried in a White Man's Court

In 1869 Lawrie Tatum, an Iowa Quaker, became agent for the Comanche and Kiowa at Fort Sill, Indian Territory. This was part of President Grant's new Quaker Policy, which turned over the Indian Bureau to representatives of religious groups. Relations with the Indians had always been handled badly; it was assumed that the new approach could be no worse than its predecessors. Tatum had had no experience in dealing with Indians and had not sought the position; he, as a Quaker, at first believed the plains tribes could be gentled by Christian and pacific treatment. He learned that the only way to halt the raids was to make the warriors responsible for their acts and in the end it was Lawrie Tatum who turned Satanta, Satank, and Big Tree over to the Army.

The Quaker policy did not improve conditions on the frontier. A Kiowa chief told Tatum the president should move Texas far away if he wanted them to stop raiding the Texans. Settlers' pleas for help were ignored by the Army until the commanding general, William T. Sherman, made an inspection tour of the frontier posts. On May 17, 1871, Sherman and General Randolph Marcy arrived at Fort Richardson. The next day a large Kiowa war party attacked Henry Warren's mule train as it was going from Jacksboro to Fort Griffin over the old Butterfield trail, the same road Sherman had traveled the day before. Seven of the twelve teamsters were killed. One of the three wounded, Thomas Brazeal, made his way to Fort Richardson to report the attack. The victims had been mutilated; Samuel Elliott was "burned to a cinder, the savages having chained the poor fellow between the wheels of a wagon and built a fire under him." For the first time Sherman admitted the existence of an Indian problem; Army policy underwent an immediate change. Sherman sent General Ranald Mackenzie and 150 cavalrymen to the scene of the massacre, and the Army surgeon reported:

> . . . I examined on May 19, 1871, the bodies . . . . All the bodies were riddled with bullets, covered with gashes, and skulls crushed . . . ; some of the bodies exhibited also signs of having been stabbed with arrows. One was found fastened with a chain to the pole of a wagon lying over a fire with the face to the ground, the tongue being cut out . . . . The scalps of all but one were taken.

While Sherman pondered his fate if the Kiowa had attacked a day earlier, a delegation from Jacksboro warned that if something were not done northwest Texas would be uninhabitable. General Marcy had probably said the same thing, for he wrote in his journal: "This rich and beautiful section of country does not contain today as many white people as it did when I was stationed here eighteen years ago, and if the Indian marauders are not punished, the whole country seems to be in a fair way of becoming depopulated."

From Fort Richardson Sherman went on to Fort Sill, arriving the day after Lawrie Tatum had written to his Quaker superiors:

Satanta, the Kiowa war chief, was tried at Jacksboro for the Salt Creek Massacre and died in the penitentiary at Huntsville.

I think the Indians . . . intend to continue their atrocities in Texas. I believe affairs will get worse until there is a different course pursued with the Indians. I know of no reason why they should not be treated the same as white people for the same offense. It is not right to be feeding and clothing them and let them raid with impunity in Texas. Will the committee sustain me in having Indians arrested for murder and turned over to the proper authorities of Texas for trial?

Sherman asked Tatum to find out if any reservation Indian had taken part in the wagon train attack. When the Indians came for rations Tatum told the chiefs what had happened and asked who had done it. Satanta said: "Yes, I led in that raid . . . . we found a mule train, which we captured, and killed seven of the men. Three of our men got killed, but we are willing to call it even . . . . " Tatum then asked Colonel Grierson, the commander of Fort Sill, to arrest Satanta, Big Tree, and others for murder.

Satanta was taken into custody and the Kiowa were summoned. Standing on Grierson's front porch Sherman asked who took part in the raid. Satanta again stated that he had led the war party. Sherman answered that it had not been a fair match, 100 warriors against 12 teamsters who did not know how to fight. When Sherman announced that Satanta, Big Tree, and Satank would have to stand trial for murder, Kicking Bird, a Kiowa chief who had attempted to keep the peace, tried to change the general's mind. About twenty soldiers were then ordered into position in front of Grierson's porch facing the Kiowa in the yard. Other soldiers were inside the house covering the Indians through the windows. One witness said:

> . . . the Indians seemed much excited, nearly all of them having either a Colt's revolver or a Spencer carbine, or both. Lone Wolf, a chief, now rode up on a fine horse, dismounted, laid two carbines and a bow and quiver of arrows on the ground, tied his horse to the fence, then throwing his blanket from his shoulders fastened it around his waist, picked up the carbines in one hand and the bow and arrow in the other, strode up to the piazza; then giving one of the carbines to an Indian who had no arms and the bow and arrows to another . . . he seated himself and cocked his carbine, at which the soldiers all brought their carbines to an aim upon the crowd, whereupon Satanta and some other Indians held up their hands and cried: "No! No! Don't Shoot!"

As Colonel Mackenzie was taking them to Jacksboro for trial Satank's actions were so threatening that he was placed in one wagon and Satanta and Big Tree in the other. Satank asked George Washington, a Caddo guide, to tell the Kiowa to come for his body, sang his death song, freed his manacled hands, and attacked the guards with one of their own rifles. He was shot and died within minutes.

Satanta and Big Tree were imprisoned at Fort Richardson on May 31. Word of their trial swept through sparsely populated northwest Texas. The Jack County grand jury indicted them, and on July 5 their trial began before Judge Charles Soward. S. W. T. Lanham, of Weatherford, who would later be governor of Texas, was the prosecutor, and Thomas Ball and Joe Woolfolk appeared for the defense. After the cases were severed Big Tree was tried first. The jury heard the testimony of the teamster Tom Brazeal, who told about the attack; a sergeant who had helped bury those killed in the battle; and Mathew Leeper, the interpreter who heard Satanta boast of having led the raid. In summation Lanham said, "This is a novel and important trial, and has perhaps no precedent in the history of American criminal jurisprudence." The eastern press, which had lauded the prisoners and objected to their trial, was referred to as:

> Indian admirers who live in more secure and favored lands remote from the frontier, where "distance lends enchantment" to the imagination, where the story of Pocahontas and the speech of Logan, the Mingo, are read, and where the sound of the warwhoop is not heard. We who see them today, disrobed of all their fancied graces, exposed in the light of reality, behold them through far different lenses!

The jury retired to an office downstairs and decided upon a verdict. Big Tree was found guilty of murder, and Judge Soward sentenced him to death by hanging.

Satanta was tried the next day, July 6. The same jury heard the case. The Fort Sill interpreter, Horace Jones, testified to Satanta's confession. The jury found him guilty. Before sentence was passed Satanta spoke through interpreter Jones; he said he was the friend of the white man and promised to keep the Kiowa out of Texas if released. Kicking Bird, Lone Wolf, and others had caused the trouble, and he would kill them if he were allowed to go, but should he be found guilty and executed, "it will be a spark on the prairie—make big fire."

A former army officer, Robert G. Carter, writing 17 years later, left this description of the event:

> The jury were all in their shirt sleeves. Each had his old "shootin iron" strapped to his hip . . . . The jury retired to a corner of the same room. A few minutes of hurried consultation and angry head shaking, and they were back again in their seats. The question was put by Judge Soward, "What say you, Mr. Foreman, is this Indian chief, Satanta, guilty, or not guilty, of murder?" The foreman said, "He is. We figger him guilty."

McConnell contradicted this account—published in Boston—in many particulars, from Carter's calling the sandstone, two-story building "a log courthouse," to the assertion that the jury was composed of armed cowboys. Weapons were not allowed in the courtroom, and most of the jurors were merchants and clerks.

Satanta and Big Tree were to hang on September 1. The judge wrote the governor urging that their sentences be commuted to life imprisonment; Governor Edmund J. Davis did so on August 2. Satanta and Big Tree arrived at Huntsville on November 12, 1871. Tatum wrote: "I had requested that the Indians not be executed, and independent of my principles against capital punishment, had given reasons for thinking that it would have a better effect on the Indians of the agency to imprison them for life."

After much agitation in the eastern press Satanta and Big Tree were paroled in October, 1873, by Governor Davis upon the promise of the Kiowa to begin farming and stop raiding. General Sherman was as appalled as those who lived on the frontier. He wrote to the governor:

> . . . that I believe Satanta and Big Tree will have their revenge if they have not already had it, and that if they are to have scalps, that yours is the first that should be taken.

When depredations increased the two were ordered back into custody. Satanta was arrested in October, 1874, and died in the Huntsville penitentiary four years later. Big Tree remained free and was still alive when the Fort Sill area was opened to homesteaders at the turn of the century.

Waco Bridged the Brazos River

Situated on the west bank of the Brazos at a spring which had served an Indian village, Waco grew into a town of 1,500 in its first dozen years. Some fording places and Captain Shapley Ross' ferry permitted access to the country east of the Brazos, except in flood season when the river was impassable. Waco's development clearly depended upon a more certain means of crossing the Brazos, which extended 870 miles from the Panhandle to the Gulf and had never been bridged.

Waco needed a bridge. Elsewhere the "Biggest Bridge in the World," spanning the Ohio River between Covington, Kentucky, and Cincinnati, was nearing completion, and its builder, John A. Roebling, was planning an even larger suspension bridge to connect New York City and Brooklyn.

Although they were short on capital, materials would have to come long distances, the closest railroad was a hundred miles away, and Federal troops occupied Texas, some Waco businessmen decided to build a bridge.

The Waco Bridge Company was chartered in November, 1866, for a term of 25 years after completion of the bridge. The company was given a bridge and ferry monopoly within five miles of Waco. Upon organization, in 1868, John T. Flint was made president of the company. A Confederate officer, lawyer, and banker, Flint was energetic and decisive. From New York Flint wrote that he had decided upon a wire cable suspension bridge, which Roebling said would cost $40,000. He was hiring the engineer; in the meantime he urged that land along the river be acquired.

Work was begun in October, 1868, and completed in late 1869. The shareholders met every call for funds and stood behind Flint, although the final cost was $141,000. The grand opening of the bridge was held January 6, 1870. Waco was filled with visitors. No longer was the Brazos an impediment to trade; traffic from a wide area funneled across the 475-foot span.

A bridge keeper was hired. Because he was on 24-hour duty a house was furnished. He paid a helper out of his $100-a-month salary. The charter established these maximum tolls; horse and rider, ten cents; wagons drawn by two animals, ten cents per wheel and five cents per animal; loose horses, mules, or cattle, five cents a head; pedestrians, five cents; and sheep, goats, or hogs, three cents each. Tolls were almost $18,000 in the first ten months. When Waco was incorporated, in 1871—the year the railroad arrived—its boundaries enclosed territory on both sides of the Brazos. A gas line and a water main were laid across the bridge. Western Union paid $25 a year to string two wires over the bridge, and Southwest Telephone paid $12 for its wire.

Opposition developed as the company forbade use of the old fording places. By 1886, voters were demanding a free bridge. After fruitless attempts to build, in 1889 McLennan County bought the original bridge for $75,000; it was then conveyed to the city, to be used without the payment of tolls.

Admirers of Waco's suspension bridge across the Brazos River called it the Magic Bridge.

Fort Sam Was a Rattlesnake Jungle

San Antonio has always been a military town. The presidio San Antonio de Bexar was established four days after the founding of the mission San Antonio de Valero in 1718. Every filibuster who coveted Spanish Texas wanted San Antonio; the Texans and Santa Anna fought for it, and when statehood came the United States located soldiers and supplies there to insure the integrity of the Mexican boundary.

The first American soldiers stationed at San Antonio, in 1846, were camped near the head of San Pedro Springs, but because this was low ground, vulnerable to attack. it was used for only a short time. After many years of occupying temporary locations, including quarters used by Spanish soldiers near the Military Plaza and the Alamo buildings, a permanent site was acquired on the edge of town; it was covered with a heavy jungle-like growth and harbored thousands of rattlesnakes.

In June, 1876, the army contracted with the Ed Braden Company for construction of the Quadrangle, which would house the quartermaster depot. The buildings were completed within the $100,000 appropriation. The Quadrangle was 624 feet square and built of soft cream-colored limestone. Three sides accomodated storerooms, and the main gate and offices were on the south side. At the center of the enclosed 7.36 acre plaza was a 15-foot square masonry tower. It was 90 feet tall and had a 6,000-gallon water tank in the top. Just below the tank, at an elevation of 65 feet, was a guardroom from which the interior of the Quadrangle and the surrounding country could be seen. A tablet on the tower serves as a reminder that U. S. Grant was president when the Quadrangle was completed, William T. Sherman was General of the Army, and Philip Sheridan commanded the division. The depot commander was Brigadier General Edward O. C. Ord, who was alleged to be a grandson of England's King George IV.

The commander of the Department of Texas moved his headquarters from the Alamo—which had been part of the mission San Antonio de Valero—into the new facilities in 1879. In the next year a hospital, 15 sets of officers quarters, and the Staff Post were planned. In 1885 the Infantry Post buildings were begun. On September 11, 1890, the installation was named Fort Sam Houston for the first president of the Republic.

The post expanded through the years. Geronimo was a prisoner there. Theodore Roosevelt's Rough Riders were supplied from Fort Sam while they prepared to go to Cuba. The Air Force had its beginnings on the Fort Sam Houston parade ground, where Lt. Benjamin Foulois assembled and flew the only airplane owned by the armed forces of the United States. The fort became the largest military post in the country and played a major part in both world wars. Its commanding officers included such great names in American military history as generals Ranald Mackenzie, John Schofield, Tasker Bliss, John Pershing, Walter Krueger, and Jonathan Wainwright. One and a half million men have been trained there.

The tower in Fort Sam Houston's Quandrangle permitted lookouts to observe inside and outside the fort.

Geronimo Was Confined at Fort Sam Houston

The Army had occupied the Quadrangle only a few years when Geronimo was held there. The Chiricahua Apache called Geronimo (Jerome) by the Mexicans was really the medicine man Goyathlay (one who yawns). Born about 1834 in New Mexico, he was raiding in Mexico in 1883 when General George Crook forced him, Nachez, Chato, and 325 other hostiles onto the San Carlos, Arizona, reservation.

Before long Geronimo and others missed the power they had formerly wielded. After trouble with the agents about tiswin, an intoxicant made from corn, Geronimo, Nachez, Chihuahua, Mangas, and 140 others fled into Mexico's Sierra Madre Mountains. After almost a year General Crook forced a surrender. The Apache had agreed to return to the reservation and Crook had departed when someone gave the Indians some whiskey. On March 27, 1886, Geronimo and Nachez escaped, taking 39 braves, women and children with them. Nachez—Nache, Natchez, or Nachi—was a chief, Geronimo was not. Nachez was Cochise's son and Mangus Colorado's grandson.

After their surrender in July, 1886, Geronimo, Nachez, and 31 others—including 17 women and children—were sent by train to exile in Florida. They stopped in San Antonio and were confined in the Quadrangle for six weeks. Visitors came to see them; Geronimo charged a dime apiece for shaking hands. They painted themselves and held dances around their bonfires in the evenings. The government provided spending money, and the Joske brothers brought goods to sell to them. They were taken on a tour, which allegedly included the Lone Star Brewery.

The *San Antonio Light* editorialized upon Geronimo's treatment:

> So great is the terror of his name in Arizona, where his bloody trail has been marked by the streams of innocent blood, that a general cry goes up to remove him beyond the boundaries of the territory, lest he escape and become again their living scourge. He is brought to this city, and how is he received? . . . . he is pampered and fed with all the luxuries of the season, fresh fruit included, while the boys in blue who perilled life in his capture are relegated to their bacon and hard tack. Bouquets have been presented him by foolishly sentimental women . . . . Was it for this purpose that the United States troops have been employed all these months? That this scalp-taker, thieving, blood-thirsty, murderous Geronimo and his band might be . . . made to feel . . . that he deserved well of the government whose citizens he had murdered in cold blood?

Geronimo, Nachez, and fourteen braves were sent to Fort Pickens, Florida, while the others went to Fort Marion, Florida, hundreds of miles away. The *Light* said, "Here in the loneliness of his island retreat, in close confinement, the old scalper will have a glorious opportunity to meditate upon his sins . . . ." The San Carlos agent reported, in 1888, "The removal of the hostile Chiricahua and Warm Springs Indians . . . has resulted very beneficially to the six remaining tribles. . . ."The Apache were moved to Alabama in 1888, then to Fort Sill; there Geronimo farmed and played celebrity for visitors. He died in February, 1909.

Geronimo, was confined at Fort Sam Houston on his way to exile in Florida.

Geronimo and fellow Apache prisoners camped in the Fort Sam Houston Quadrangle.

Geronimo, in top hat, drove an automobile at the 101 Ranch during a 1905 convention.

Oil Springs Was the First Texas Field

The first recorded use of Texas petroleum occurred in 1543 when survivors of the De Soto expedition calked the bottom of their boats with a heavy black substance they found near Sabine Pass. The Indians were aware of petroleum seepages. In the late 18th century Antonio Gil Ybarbo used oil skimmed from a Nacogdoches County creek for medicinal purposes. In 1859 Jack Graham dug the state's first oil well, which was only a pit near an Angelina County tar spring that filled with water and oil.

Soon after the close of the Civil War, Lynis T. Barret, trying to obtain greater quantities of oil than could be skimmed from a pond near Melrose, dug Texas' first real oil well. At 106 feet, drilling with an auger powered by a steam engine, he found oil; the Nacogdoches County well yielded ten barrels a day. After capping the well Barret went to Pennsylvania for financial and technical aid. John F. Carl brought his equipment to Texas, drilled an 80-foot well with Barret, and gave up. Too many good drilling sites were still available in Pennsylvania, and Nacogdoches County was near no substantial market. For those same reasons Barret could not get other assistance.

Others, including Civil War hero Dick Dowling, became interested in drilling near oil seepages, with no appreciable results. Martin Meichinger, digging a Brownwood water well, found oil, which he bottled and sold as medicine. Some minor gas discoveries were also being made. One well near Palo Pinto ignited and produced a forty-foot flame; the owner had the hole filled in, explaining that he was "hunting for water, not fire."

This activity caused some national companies to consider drilling in Texas, which revived interest in the oil spring at Nacogdoches. In 1886 E. F. Hitchcock brought in the well that precipitated the first Texas boom. Drilled with a cable tool near the oil spring, it flowed some 250 barrels the first day from a depth of 70 feet. Although the flow then ceased, the strike generated excitement and attracted oil men and crews from Pennsylvania. Wooden storage tanks were used initially, and then the first steel tanks and the first pipeline in Texas were built. The Lubricating Oil Company, which drilled about three miles from the oil spring, did Texas' first refining. Production from their wells was by use of buckets ten or fifteen feet long which brought up oil and water. The buckets were emptied into a barrel and the oil drawn off the water; the refining process evaporated whatever water remained.

About 90 wells were drilled, and for a time 150 men were employed in the Oil Springs Field, but most of the activity was over by 1891. Many had come there from Pennsylvania because of declining production; as the eastern fields revived, in 1890, they left Texas. The pipeline from the Oil Springs Field was later taken up and part of it was used in the Nacogdoches water system.

The Nacogdoches County oil spring was an obvious place to prospect for petroleum.

Elisabet Ney Sculpted Schopenhauer

Elisabet Ney was born January 26, 1833, in Munster, Westphalia, Germany. Her mother was Polish and her father was a nephew of Napoleon's Marshal Ney. Early in life she decided to be a sculptress, then an unusual ambition for a woman. At the age of eighteen she went to Munich, sought admission to the Academy of Art, and was rejected at first; it was feared that her presence would distract the all-male student body. After she was admitted, a professor was assigned to accompany her to and from classes.

She went to Berlin in 1854 to study under master sculptor Christian Rauch and entered the Berlin Academy of Art. In Berlin she met a number of distinguished individuals who assisted her in finding subjects. She approached the philosopher Arthur Schopenhauer, and although he had little regard for women, he did sit for her. The bust of Schopenhauer, who was one of the great men of the time, guaranteed her success. In the next few years Miss Ney executed busts of Jacob Grimm, scholar and writer of fairy tales, Alexander von Humboldt, King George V of Hanover, King Ludwig of Bavaria, Wagner, Garibaldi, Bismarck, and others of high rank.

Miss Ney, while she was a student in Munich, had met Edmund Montgomery during a visit to Heidelberg. He was a Scot and a medical student. After receiving his degree he began practice as a physician in London where he contracted tuberculosis; he and Miss Ney married November 7, 1863, and lived on the island of Madeira off the coast of Spain for the next few years. Dr. Montgomery was conducting scientific experiments and writing philosophy while practicing medicine. A bequest made it possible for him to devote most of his time to experimentation and philosophy.

In 1871 they came to the United States and settled at Thomasville, Georgia, where the climate was supposed to be beneficial for the tubercular. Accompanying them was Cencie Simath, their housekeeper, who remained with them for the rest of their lives. Miss Ney managed their farm while Dr. Montgomery carried on his scientific and philosophic work. The neighbors did not know what to think of them. Miss Ney offered no explanation for her refusal to use her husband's name; in addition she wore bloomers, boots, a man's coat, and carried a cane. Her first child, Arthur, born in Georgia, was named for Schopenhauer.

Miss Ney practiced no sculpture in Georgia, nor did she resume her art after coming to Waller County, Texas, in 1873. Dr. Montgomery bought the Liendo plantation from Leonard Groce, and there Arthur Montgomery, two years old, died. Miss Ney could not bear the thought of his burial, so he was cremated in the fireplace of the Liendo mansion. His ashes remained unburied until they were placed inside Dr. Montgomery's coffin many years later.

At Liendo, Miss Ney took charge of the field work, as she had done in Georgia. Although the farm operation was usually unprofitable she kept buying more land. Her manner of dress, use of her maiden name, her foreign origins, and the role she assumed were strange to Waller County. Her unwillingness to allow her son, Lorne, to associate with other children provoked them. Lorne was spoiled by his mother at the same time his life was complicated by the community's belief that his parents were not married. Miss Ney dressed him in flowing white robes and other alien costumes. The result was Lorne's rebellion and lifelong estrangement from his mother.

Elisabet Ney built a studio in Austin which she named Formosa.

Along the way Miss Ney had met Oran Roberts. As governor, Roberts, interested in building a new capitol, sought her counsel. She advised against the statuary he had planned and urged that the structure be built of red granite. After Lorne was sent to school in Philadelphia, in 1886, Miss Ney's interest in sculpture revived. Turning the management of Liendo over to Dr. Montgomery, she began spending time in Austin, a town of only 10,000 residents but still the state capital and the site of the new university. There she hoped to practice her art again. Little painting was being done in Texas and no sculpture worthy of the name.

Planning for the Chicago World's Fair, the Columbian Exposition, to be held in 1893, Governor Roberts, then a University of Texas law professor, suggested that Miss Ney be commissioned to do the statuary for the Texas building. Although the committee did not have enough money to pay her she welcomed the opportunity. She would execute plaster statues of Stephen F. Austin and Sam Houston. Perhaps funds would be available later to have them done in marble and to compensate her.

At first Miss Ney worked in the basement of the new capitol, which was not suitable for use as a studio. As a consequence only the Houston statue was ready when the fair opened; however, it attracted much attention in Chicago, both because of its quality and surprise that such work had been done in Texas. The interest generated by her success at the fair enabled Miss Ney to build an Austin studio, which she named Formosa. Praise for achievement in the arts was a novel experience for Texans, and many who wanted artistic recognition for the state worked in her behalf. Supporters frequented the studio and promoted commissions for Miss Ney, hoping she would form the nucleus of a community of artists and patrons.

Because only a few individuals able to patronize sculptors were interested in doing so, her partisans decided the state would have to provide a market. The first step was to get the legislature to finance marble statues of the Houston and Austin plaster models; one set would be placed in the statehouse and the other in the capitol rotunda at Washington where each state could exhibit statues of two citizens. The campaign was a long, hard, bitter one. Legislators feared their constituents would consider them wasteful, and they offered every conceivable objection. For instance, if Miss Ney were such a fine sculptress how could she live for two decades in Texas without anyone becoming aware of her talents? Furthermore, who ever heard of a woman carving statues? And who needed statues anyway?

The resistance precipitated personal attacks; there had to be something wrong with a woman who dressed as Miss Ney did. Her apparel never coincided with prevailing fashion. All of the Waller County suspicions were imported. Obviously she was without morals, the gossip went, a condition which had caused the estrangement of her son.

In the meantime she had done busts of governors Roberts, Lubbock, and Ross, and Senator Reagan; these she took to Germany in 1895. It was important to her to learn what had been happening in the world of art during the past twenty years. While she was in Europe her champions began to make progress. Mrs. Joseph Dibrell, of Seguin, the chairman of the Ney committee and wife of a state senator, persuaded her husband to help. Senator Dibrell was successful, and in 1901 an appropriation was made for the Houston and Austin pieces. Then the legislature authorized a statue of General Albert Sidney Johnston for the state cemetery. The statues of Houston and Austin were unveiled in January, 1903. Miss Ney executed other works for the state and the university. She made two more trips to Europe to superintend the carving of the Johnston piece and others. Her statue of Lady Macbeth was done when Miss Ney was nearly seventy years old.

Philosopher Arthur Schopenhauer's agreement to sit for her launched Elisabet Ney's career.

Through the years Dr. Montgomery had tried to sell Liendo. He came to Austin occasionally, but while they were apart they corresponded almost daily.

Mrs. Taylor, in her fine volume, says of Miss Ney:

> Unfortunate it was for her that those years of her prime which should have been the richest in production were fated to be wasted in surroundings which made creative work impossible . . . for those years of her greatest unhappiness at Liendo when she was straining so uselessly against the restraints of her unfavorable environment were exactly the dawn of American sculpture . . . . Even to think of her in contact with the artists who during those years laid the foundation for what has since reached such a splendid culmination is to feel certain that both she and our national art would have been the gainers.

Because of her isolation in Texas art critics were not aware of her. Lorado Taft discovered her work by chance when he visited Texas on a lecture tour. Of the recumbent statue of General Johnston, which she was just completing, he wrote, "This is a work of high order, as is the promise of a sketch of Lady Macbeth—one of the most expressive and eminently sculptural conceptions among recent American ideals."

Miss Ney produced some 100 works during her career. Bronchial difficulties from breathing marble dust while supervising the carving of the Johnston piece in Italy aggravated a heart condition, and she died at Formosa on June 29, 1907. Dr. Montgomery died April 17, 1911. Both are buried at Liendo.

Miss Ney had wanted the University of Texas to have her sculptures, but lack of funds made that difficult. Mrs. Dibrell bought Formosa to assist Dr. Montgomery financially and to convert it into a museum for Miss Ney's collection. The university accepted the statuary upon the condition that it have no obligation for care and maintenance. The Texas Fine Arts Association was formed in April, 1911, to manage Formosa and exhibit the collection. Formosa is now operated by the Austin Parks and Recreation Department.

Miss Ney's Lady Macbeth may have been her best work.

Elisabet Ney executed a self-portrait at Formosa.

The finished statues of Stephen F. Austin stand in the national and state capitols.

The Corsicana Strike Was the Prologue to Spindletop

Water-well drillers at Corsicana in June, 1894, found petroleum at about a thousand feet; using casing to close it off they continued on to water at 2,470 feet, but the oil came up the outside of the casing in sufficient quantities to attract attention. Although there was only slight demand for oil in Texas, a company was formed to prospect in Corsicana, its founders believing markets could be developed. J. M. Guffey and John Galey, who had been successful in the Pennsylvania fields, were induced to drill five wells. Two hundred feet from the water well they struck oil at 1,030 feet; the well flowed two and a half barrels a day. Their second attempt was a dry hole. Number three, at Fourth and Collins, yielded 22 barrels a day. The wells were all small producers but were sufficiently exciting in that pre-gusher era. Oil companies multiplied, and wells were drilled throughout Corsicana, on vacant lots, in front yards, and in back yards. Men from the older oil-producing states poured into town, and leasing and drilling extended beyond the city limits. Of 57 wells completed in 1897, only seven were dusters. The record was better in the next year when there were 25 failures in 316 attempts.

The production quickly saturated the tiny local market. Had the wells been in Pennsylvania the oil would have brought a dollar a barrel, but the eastern markets were far away; Corsicana oil sold for much less, if a buyer could be found. Part of the problem was solved by J. S. Cullinan's arrival in Corsicana. His firm, which later became the Magnolia Petroleum Company, built the first commercial refinery in Texas. There the illuminating oil and gasoline were extracted—the residue was used to fuel the drilling rigs and the refinery—and shipped out by rail. As the price of local crude went up, more wells were drilled. Cullinan, seeking new customers, persuaded the Cotton Belt railroad to substitute oil for coal in their locomotives, an innovation which created huge demands for petroleum as railroads converted to oil burners. The Corsicana field produced 65,975 barrels in 1897, 546,070 in 1898, 669,813 in 1899, and 836,039 in 1900.

The most important results of the Corsicana strike were: (1) the passage of conservation legislation curtailing some of the wasteful practices which developed in that field, (2) proof that Texas had substantial quantities of oil, and (3) the introduction into the state of men experienced in oil exploration. The Corsicana field was the prologue to the single most important event in petroleum history, the Spindletop gusher. Because Corsicana oil had been found in paying quantities, Guffey and Galey would back Andy Lucas at Beaumont. Because the Hamill brothers had developed their skills at Corsicana they would be able to solve the technical problems they would encounter at the Beaumont well.

THE BIRTHPLACE OF THE
PETROLEUM INDUSTRY

WEST OF THE MISSISSIPPI RIVER • IN
THIS WELL, DRILLED BY H. G. JOHNSTON,
E. H. AKIN, AND CHARLES RITTERSBACHER
UNDER CONTRACT FOR A WATER WELL
FOR THE CITY OF CORSICANA IN
1894, THE FIRST OIL IN COMMERCIAL
QUANTITIES IN THE MID-CONTINENT
AREA WAS DISCOVERED AT 1035 FEET

Erected by the State of Texas
1936

The drilling of a Corsicana water well made Texas an oil-producing state.

The Twentieth Century Came in at Beaumont

Pattillo Higgins became interested in Beaumont's Big Hill when he was a young man. Once when he took his Sunday School class on a picnic there Higgins stuck a cane into the earth and set fire to the escaping gas to entertain the children. From the hill came several kinds of mineral water which were used for medicinal purposes; actually it was only a mound which rose about 15 feet above the surrounding plain. Higgins studied geology and decided there were vast quantities of oil beneath the Big Hill.

In 1892, some friends joined Higgins in forming the Gladys City Oil, Gas and Manufacturing Company, which he named for Gladys Bingham, a member of his Sunday School class. Two contracts were let for the drilling of wells on the Big Hill in spite of Higgins' protests that the contractors' equipment was too light; Higgins claimed oil would be found at 1,000 feet. Although neither attempt reached 500 feet, the dry holes discouraged Higgins' associates; disgusted with their failure to do what was necessary, Higgins left the company but retained some of his leases on the Big Hill. The assistant state geologist came to Beaumont and reported that there was no possibility of oil there. Through the years Higgins' efforts to get a suitable well drilled, made him a local joke. Those who ridiculed his idea called him "the millionaire."

Knowing there was no possibility of local support, Higgins ran an advertisement in an engineering journal. He got one reply, but that was enough; Anthony Lucas thought there was a chance for sulphur production at the Big Hill. By the time Lucas arrived in Beaumont, Higgins still had only 33 acres on the hill and a few lots in the adjoining Gladys City addition, but Higgins had the right man. Antonio Luchich had graduated from the Austrian Naval Academy and was a navy lieutenant when he came to Michigan to visit an uncle. He remained in the United States, became a citizen, and changed his name. During his years as a mining engineer he developed a theory that oil and sulphur accumulate around salt domes. He wanted the sulphur beneath the hill, which was in fact a salt dome. Higgins was given a 10% interest in Lucas' contracts.

Lucas began drilling in July, 1899. His rotary rig was too light, but before he abandoned the hole he found a small quantity of heavy crude. With this sample he persuaded the Standard Oil Company to evaluate the prospects; however, Standard's chief geologist, after visiting the site, stated, "You will never find oil here." Other experts, private and federal, had the same opinion, convincing neither Lucas nor Higgins. The only geologist who gave any encouragement was Dr. William Battle Phillips of the University of Texas; he put Lucas in touch with James Guffey and John Galey.

Galey and Guffey, who had prospered at Corsicana, agreed to back Lucas in another well; Lucas was to lease as much of the area as possible. Galey went to the hill and marked the place where the well was to be sunk; it was near the rough sulphur-water vats in which farmers dipped hogs to cure mange and kill fleas. The Hamill brothers, Curt, Al, and Jim, were hired to drill the well, which was begun October 26, 1900. There occurred several novel problems for which the Hamills had

Pattillo Higgins' interest in the Big Hill near Beaumont changed the history of the world.

to find solutions. On January 9, 1901, they were having trouble penetrating a rock formation into which they had already drilled 140 feet; at 1020 feet it appeared that the bit was hitting a crevice and making no headway while the drill stem seemed about to break. On the following morning the stem was pulled and a new bit was mounted. Some 700 feet of drill stem had been lowered into the hole when suddenly mud began spurting high up into the derrick. Curt Hamill and his two employees ran for safety, then six tons of drill stem shot through the top of the derrick and broke into sections as it fell. The men had approached the well to assess the damage when, at 10:30 a.m., a deafening roar began. Mud, gas, and, finally, heavy crude oil shot 200 feet into the air, coming from 1020 feet below the surface, less than seven yards from where Higgins said it would be.

When Lucas reached the site he could not believe what he saw—only a few people in Russia's Baku field had ever seen the world's other gusher—and he yelled to Al Hamill over the roar, "What is it?" The driller shouted, "Oil, Captain! Oil, every drop of it."

Lucas stared at the black spout and said, "A geyser of oil. A geyser of oil!"

Everyone in the vicinity came to see the spectacle, and word went out by telegraph to the entire world. When Pattillo Higgins returned from a trip that afternoon and did not appear surprised by the news, he reminded his informant, "Don't you remember that I've been telling everyone for more than ten years that this would happen?"

Crowds poured into Beaumont to buy and sell leases, to seek work, or simply to see the geyser—or gusher—which was flowing at nearly 100,000 barrels a day. Farmers had been hired to build dikes for the lake of oil that was accumulating and running into the Neches River. Guards were hired to keep the spectators back. Lucas was afraid a smoker might start a fire, which did, in fact, occur on Sunday. Fortunately he and some volunteers were able to stop that conflagration before much damage was done, but Lucas' concern increased as the well continued out of control. Offers to cap the well—for a price—were coming in from all over the nation.

The Hamills rigged an apparatus upon which an open valve was mounted. They intended to move the valve in over the flow, nail the heavy mounting to the legs of the derrick, and then close the valve. For protection from the oil, gas, and deafening noise they devised goggles, masks, and heavy earplugs. Teams of mules were used to drag the apparatus into place. The contraption worked. After nine days the gusher was quiet; the derrick stood in a sea of almost one million barrels of green crude.

The next step was to protect the well from fire. S. L. Battle, who ran a Beaumont tin shop, said:

> On Saturday, January 19, Captain Lucas came to my shop and contracted with me to make the well he had bored "fool and fire proof." I built an iron cylinder eight feet in diameter and eight feet high, carried it to the Big Hill, and placed it over the well, then filled it with dry sand. I worked all night Saturday and until noon Sunday.

Storage and transportation facilities were needed to get the oil off the ground and to take the well's flow. Beaumont's population grew from 9,000 to 50,000 within weeks. Men slept wherever they could, some buying 30-day Pullman tickets so they could ride to Houston in the afternoon and sleep on the train as it returned to Beaumont the next morning. Armies of speculators arrived to buy and sell leases in the Spindletop field, so called because a tall cypress tree, a landmark in the vicinity of the Big Hill, had once been compared to an inverted spindletop. Land that had brought $20 an acre was now worth $50,000.

The Lucas gusher at Beaumont's Big Hill demonstrated that petroleum would be the fuel of the twentieth century.

Lucas' safety precautions paid off when, on March 3, sparks from a passing locomotive ignited the sea of oil. Within a few hours 900,000 barrels of petroleum was consumed. But the well was not harmed.

The significance of the Spindletop discovery was, as the former mayor of Toledo, Ohio, Samuel M. (Golden Rule) Jones, claimed, "Liquid petroleum is destined to be the fuel of the twentieth century." Until then coal had been the main source of industrial energy. It had been assumed that there was no more petroleum beneath the earth than was needed for illumination and lubrication. Russia was the leading oil producing country, but its wells had little impact on the world since they were located 600 miles from ocean transport.

In the United States 58 million barrels of oil were produced in 1900, of which the Corsicana wells had yielded only a million. The Lucas gusher produced more than twice as much oil as the nation's leading oil state, Pennsylvania. After the next five gushers came in, the Spindletop field was producing more oil than the rest of the world's wells combined, serving notice that there was enough petroleum beneath the earth to power the new horseless carriages, locomotives, ships, factories, and whatever else men might require in the new century.

A granite shaft marks the site of the Lucas gusher.

145

Fort Worth Became a Packing Center

Since it was the last town of consequence before the long drive across the Indian Territory to Kansas, Fort Worth became an important place to cowhands and cattlemen. After the arrival of the railroad in 1876, W. T. Waggoner, Burk Burnett, and other West Texas ranchers made Fort Worth their headquarters.

Once refrigerated freight cars were developed Fort Worth became a natural place for packing plants. Substantial savings could be realized by shipping dressed beef instead of cattle to market. Furthermore, local packing facilities would help cattlemen maintain prices and solve the fever problem. Texas trail herds had encountered opposition because of a fever-producing tick carried by the cattle. The longhorns were immune, but the fever was deadly to other cattle. Dressed beef carried no ticks.

Issac Dahlman pioneered the packing business in Fort Worth. After years of effort he filled his first large order in 1890, slaughtering some 300 head. Unfortunately, the ship's refrigeration system failed and the beef spoiled between Galveston and Liverpool. A new firm, the Texas Dressed Beef and Packing Company, bought the Dahlman plant. Because it was not properly managed, L. V. Niles took charge in 1893. He operated at a profit but could not handle the volume as herds poured into Fort Worth. J. Ogden Armour, whose father had founded Chicago's Armour and Company, investigated the prospects and decided to build a plant. Niles persuaded Swift and Company to join Armour in Fort Worth. Their plans were contingent upon local help in building their facilities, but by October 7, 1901, citizens had raised the necessary $100,000.

The new plants were built on the land of the Texas Dressed Beef company. Railroad tracks were extended and construction was begun in early 1902. To keep Fort Worth from annexing the land and subjecting the plants to city taxes, the area was later incorporated as Niles City. The first cattle were processed by Swift and Armour in March, 1903. Some 375,000 head of cattle reached Fort Worth that year, nearly three times the 1902 volume. The plants' operating capacity was about 150 head per hour at first. Since the beef profit margin was low, 2,000 different by-products were made, including soap, glue, drugs, and fertilizer. The plants employed 10,000 when unionization began. A strike occurred in December, 1921. As violence broke out, Fort Worth police could only stand outside the boundary of the mile-square Niles City and watch; the inadequacy of the nine-man Niles City police force during the strike later figured in Fort Worth's annexation of the area. In the disorder a Negro, Fred Rouse, was wounded after shooting two Swift employees. On December 11, he was taken from a Fort Worth hospital and lynched.

At their peak Armour and Swift processed 300 animals per hour. As transportation improved, smaller, more efficient plants were built nearer the ranches, and Fort Worth's cattle volume fell. Because their plants required extensive modernization to remain competitive Armour and Swift curtailed operations. The Armour plant closed in 1962 and Swift a few years thereafter.

The Fort Worth Livestock Exchange supplied cattle to the packing houses.

The Stockyards Were a Cattle Hotel

As the trail drives passed through Fort Worth herds were permitted to graze along the Trinity while the cowhands enjoyed the pleasures of the town. After the railroad arrived corrals and chutes were built to confine and load cattle. When the packing plants began operations, permanent stockyards were needed to hold the animals pending processing. Officers of the Fort Worth Dressed Meat and Packing Company, in 1893, organized the firm which became the Fort Worth Stockyards Company to operate the pens. When Armour and Swift came to Fort Worth they acquired interests in the stockyards; J. Ogden Armour became president and E. F. Swift vice president. After Congress prohibited packer ownership of stockyards in 1921 Armour and Swift sold their shares and then contracted with the stockyards company to handle the cattle processed through their plants.

The sole function of the stockyard was to maintain the cattle until they were needed. Each animal was registered, corraled, and fed, for which the owner paid a fee. Dipping or spraying was available, as were veterinary services. Records were kept on all animals passing through the yards, reflecting weights and conditions, sale prices, buyers, sellers, and dates of sale. At first the yards could handle 5,000 animals; they were expanded to a capacity of 13,000 in 1904. As truck transport increased cattle arrived in smaller numbers than had been the case with rail shipments, causing cattle to move through the yards more rapidly; most did not remain there overnight.

Sales were handled by agents, to whom the owners consigned the cattle and paid a commission. Agents would show the animals to potential buyers and note their bids, which were kept confidential. Sales were made to the highest bidders. Armour and Swift made most of the purchases, but many sales were to ranchers building herds or to feedlot operators.

The Fort Worth Stockyard was the first major terminal to hold public auctions. While private sales continued to be made, the auction permitted cattle to be sold for the highest bid in open competition. Commission agents handled these sales also. A small fee was charged for use of the auction facilities.

The peak years for the Fort Worth yards came during the two world wars. In 1948 Fort Worth ranked seventh in volume nationally, but 20 years later, after the closing of the Armour plant and during Swift's decline, Fort Worth held 29th place. Motor scooters were used to handle the cattle in the yards.

Through the years the Southwestern Exposition and Fat Stock Show was held to promote the cattle industry. Both Swift and Armour contributed funds to build the North Side Coliseum in 1908, and the world's first indoor rodeo was held there in 1919. The exposition had outgrown the facilities at the stockyards by 1944, when it was moved to Will Rogers Memorial Coliseum.

The stockyards held cattle pending processing by Armour and Swift plants at the end of this street.

Jack Abernathy Caught Wolves with His Hands

John Abernathy, born in Bosque County, began working as a cowhand when he was only a boy. He attended school for a few years, then moved to the Panhandle. At sixteen Abernathy was breaking horses on Charles Goodnight's JA Ranch, gentling two broncos each morning and two every afternoon. He caught his first wolf while working for the JA. His dogs had cornered a big "loafer" wolf, which was getting the best of them, and Abernathy intervened to save the dogs. His left arm was badly bitten, and accidentally he put his right hand into the wolf's mouth. To Abernathy's amazement the wolf was unable to bite as long as he gripped its lower jaw. Abernathy took the 127-pound wolf home alive.

After a few months of riding wild horses and catching wolves Abernathy decided to become a musician. At seventeen he entered Peterson's Institute in Hillsboro to study the piano and was immediately aware of the professor's niece, Pearl Jordan, who was a few months younger than he was. When Professor Taliaferro took over Ball College, in Galveston, Abernathy followed. He and Pearl eloped when he was barely eighteen. He sold pianos in Fort Worth for awhile, and they lived in Greer County before settling near Frederick, Oklahoma Territory.

Abernathy was a peace officer and sold wolves to zoos, parks, and traveling shows. Colonel Cecil A. Lyon hired Abernathy to catch wolves in an exhibition at his rabbit-racing park near Sherman in December, 1904. Colonel Lyon, a wealthy lumber and hardware dealer, was the Republican National Committeeman for Texas. On Christmas Day, Abernathy had caught several wolves without difficulty, but just before making his last run he drank some whiskey. As he started to grab the wolf Abernathy glanced away, and the animal bit him several times before Abernathy could subdue him. He wrote that the liquor had affected his timing, and he vowed never to make that mistake again.

During his career Abernathy caught more than a thousand wolves with his hands. He wrote:

> Usually I wore a thin glove—the thinner the better. I wore this glove merely to prevent the sharp canine teeth of the wolf from splitting open the skin on my hand. In thrusting my hand into the mouth of a biting wolf sometimes the sharp teeth would scratch the skin if I didn't have on a thin glove . . . . If I had used thick gloves, it would have made the job more difficult . . . .

Abernathy tried to teach others, without success.

> Nearly all were able to make the catch so far as letting the wolf have their hand. But when the savage animal would clamp down on the hand the student would become frightened, fearing the hand would be forever ruined. Instead of holding fast to the lower jaw and taking a harmless pinch, the student would quit. Consequently the wolf then would almost ruin the hand. In nearly every case the student was bitten badly and it was up to me to catch the wolf.

—Temple Abernathy

Jack Abernathy on his wolf-hunting horse, Sam Bass.

Theodore Roosevelt Came to Texas for a Wolf Hunt

One month after Theodore Roosevelt began his second term he was in Sherman on his way to a wolf hunt promoted by Colonel Cecil A. Lyon. Roosevelt had come to see Jack Abernathy catch wolves barehanded. The hunt was originally planned for the north Texas ranches of Tom Waggoner and Burk Burnett, but Abernathy had it moved across the Red River where there was not much mesquite.

Texas Governor S. W. T. Lanham, who had begun his career prosecuting Satanta, had worried about the president's safety; the hunt's taking place in Oklahoma made no difference. Lanham assigned Ranger Captain Bill McDonald to guard Theodore Roosevelt. At Fort Worth twenty thousand met him at the T & P station, and more filled the streets as he went by carriage to plant a tree at the Carnegie Library, Ninth and Throckmorton. As well-wishers swept past the Secret Service men at Wichita Falls, McDonald halted them; he had handled a lynch mob there nine years before, and some remembered. From Frederick, Oklahoma Territory, the Secret Service agents returned to Fort Worth, and the party started by horse for the campsite, 25 miles west in the Comanche big pasture.

The group included Tom Waggoner, Burk Burnett, Tom Burnett, Lieutenant General S. M. B. Young—called "War Bonnet" by the Indians—Cecil Lyon, Dallas postmaster Sloan Simpson, Quanah Parker, the last war chief of the Quahadi Comanche, and about ten others. Burk Burnett and General Young followed the chase by buggy, and dogs not used in a particular run traveled by wagon.

The hunters would be coursing mainly prairie wolves, or coyotes, weighing about 32 pounds, killers of sheep and calves. A few days earlier Abernathy had captured a sixty-pound black wolf. Zoos paid fifty dollars apiece for the animals he sent them. The president was immediately impressed by Abernathy; at the end of a ten-mile chase, this is what Roosevelt saw:

> The coyote was obviously tired, and Abernethy (the president never spelled Abernathy's name correctly, and he called his hosts, Tom Waggoner, "Mr. Wagner," and Burk Burnett, "Burke") with the aid of his perfectly trained horse, was helping the greyhound catch it. Twice he headed it, and this enabled me to gain rapidly. They had reached a small unwooded creek by the time I was within fifty yards; the little wolf tried to break back to the left; Abernethy headed it and rode almost over it, and it gave a wicked snap at his foot, cutting the boot .... just as it crossed the creek the greyhound made a rush, pinned it by the hind leg and threw it. There was a scuffle, then a yell from the greyhound as the wolf bit it. At the bite the hound let go and jumped back a few feet, and at the same moment Abernethy, who had ridden his horse right on them as they struggled, leaped off and sprang on top of the wolf. He held the reins of the horse with one hand and thrust the other, with a rapidity and precision even greater than the rapidity of the wolf's snap, into the wolf's mouth, jamming his hand down crosswise between the jaws, seizing the lower jaw and bending it down so the wolf could not bite him. He had a stout glove on his hand, but this would have been of no avail whatever had he not seized the animal just

A mighty throng greeted President Theodore Roosevelt at the Grayson County courthouse as he arrived for the wolf hunt arranged by Col. Cecil Lyon, of Sherman.

as he did; that is, behind the canines, while his hand pressed the lips against the teeth; with his knees he kept the wolf from using its forepaws to break the hold until it gave up struggling. When he thus leaped on and captured this coyote it was entirely free, the dog having let go of it; and he was obliged to keep hold of the reins of the horse with one hand. I was not twenty yards distant at the time; and as I leaped off the horse he was sitting placidly on the live wolf, his hand between its jaws, the greyhound standing beside him, and his horse standing by as placid as he was . . . . It was as remarkable a feat of the kind as I have ever seen.

Abernathy then realized he had brought nothing with which to tie the wolf's muzzle.

However, Abernethy regarded the lack of the straps as nothing more than a slight bother. Asking one of us to hold his horse, he threw the wolf across in front of the saddle, still keeping his grip on the jaw, then mounted and rode off with us on the back track. The wolf was not tied in any way. It was unhurt, and the only hold he had was on its lower jaw.

When Roosevelt asked about his technique, Abernathy said, "Well, Mr. President, you must remember that a wolf never misses its aim when it snaps. When I strike at a wolf with my right hand I know it is going into the wolf's mouth."

Abernathy's example stimulated two hunters to similar efforts; they got mangled hands for their trouble. Roosevelt had considered trying an Abernathy catch, but now he directed his ambitions elsewhere. Seeing a large rattler coiled and ready to strike, he jumped off his horse and attacked with a small riding quirt. As the snake struck, the president dodged and hit it with the quirt. With his boot heel he finished the rattlesnake, which was five feet long and as big around as a man's wrist. After Roosevelt subdued a second rattler, McDonald became frightened for his safety; that night McDonald threw the quirt into the campfire, aware that its loss would cause extreme presidential pique the next morning when the snake war was to continue.

Quanah Parker's wives, Tonarcy and two others, arrived on the second day. The chase, was described as ". . . . a genuine jubilee when a coyote was started up and followed by that boisterous company, the buggy of 'War Bonnet' and Burnett hitting only the high places; Too-Nicey and her matrimonial alliance bouncing along in the hack, with the dog-wagon, wildly excited—a regular canine explosion—bringing up the rear."

Each evening the company gathered around the campfire, and Quanah told the president of his life as a Comanche chieftain, of his mother, Cynthia Ann Parker, and of his father, Peta Nocona, singing his death song and dying a warrior's death. A few months later Roosevelt made Jack Abernathy the United States Marshal for the Oklahoma Territory.

Texas cattle barons W. T. Waggoner and Burk Burnett hosted a wolf hunt in the Comanche Big Pasture, Oklahoma Territory, so Theodore Roosevelt could see Jack Abernathy catch wolves. Standing: Panhandle rancher Lee Bivens, Texas Ranger Captain Bill McDonald, Abernathy, General S.M.B. Young, Burk Burnett, Roosevelt, E. M. Gillis. Seated: a soldier, Bony More, Guy Waggoner, Comanche Chief Quanah Parker, Republican National Committeeman for Texas Cecil Lyon, Dr. Alexander Lambert, the president's physician, D. P. Taylor. Not shown: W. T. Waggoner and Dallas postmaster Sloan Simpson.

155

The Abernathy Boys Rode Horses from New York to San Francisco

Mrs. John Abernathy died in 1907, when her sons were quite young; Louie Van had been born in Tarrant County, Texas, December 17, 1899, and Temple Reeves was born in the Oklahoma Territory on March 25, 1904. They were raised to be as independent and self-reliant as their father; Jack Abernathy had worked cattle from the time he was seven years old and at eleven he made a 500-mile trail drive. He took eighteen-month-old Temple wolf-hunting—holding the boy in front of him in the saddle as his horse raced wolves. Louie rode from his fourth year. In 1905 Louie was introduced to Theodore Roosevelt as the president came to the Comanche country to see Jack Abernathy catch wolves.

When Louie was nine and Temple was five they rode by themselves from their Guthrie, Oklahoma, home down to Frederick and then out to Santa Fe. Louie was riding Sam Bass, his father's wolf-hunting horse, and Temple rode Geronimo. The year was 1909, and their father, the United States Marshal for Oklahoma, was in New Mexico to deliver some prisoners. They carried very little food and only a few dollars because, as Louie said:

> My father gave me a checkbook. He didn't want us to carry a lot of money. Somebody might take it away from us. But I never had anybody refuse to cash a check and I didn't have to give many. We could stay in a hotel for a dollar, if we needed to, and nine times out of ten they would keep the check for a souvenir, not cash it. Mostly we stayed at farm houses and ranch houses, and they wouldn't take money from a couple of kids riding across the country.

After a few days in Santa Fe they returned to Guthrie. The only trouble on this or their later trips was Sam Bass wanting to chase every wolf he saw and Temple's over-indulgence in "red sody pop" when available. Louie remembered, "Of course we went in swimming every time we came to a puddle of water." Temple was not big enough to saddle his horse; Louie did that for him, but Temple had to mount by himself. "I don't know how he did it. There are straps and things to climb up with. All I know is I didn't help him."

The 2,000-mile Santa Fe trip whetted their taste for travel. In the following summer Theodore Roosevelt was to return from an African safari; Jack Abernathy intended to meet his ship, so Louie and Temple decided to ride Sam Bass and Geronimo to New York City to greet the former president. They left in early April, 1910, taking a change of clothes, extra blankets, and some bacon and bread. Because they would travel through more heavily settled country, Louie carried a letter signed by his father stating that they were not runaways.

They stopped first in Oklahoma City. At Hominy, on the Osage reservation, Geronimo went lame, and Louie bought for Temple a young, spotted horse that had been ridden only once before. Temple named him Wylie Haynes after one of his father's deputies. After Temple rode Wylie Haynes long enough to settle him down, they headed for Kansas. In the mountains near Springfield, Missouri, a cold rain turned to sleet and snow. To keep from freezing they had to walk beside the horses. Finally reaching a town, they spent a day in a hotel while the snowstorm continued, then went on to St. Louis.

Temple Abernathy, left, and Louie Abernathy, right, in Amarillo on their 2,000 mile trip from Guthrie, Oklahoma, to Santa Fe, New Mexico.

They were receiving so much publicity that officials welcomed them at almost every major city. Louie wrote from St. Louis that they rode in the mayor's car and met Governor Hadley and a former Missouri governor. As they crossed Illinois, Indiana, and Ohio, the crowds increased and the boys had to guard against souvenir hunters who pulled out the horses' tails and manes. At Dayton they met Wilbur Wright and toured his new factory; he and his brother had flown the first airplane only a few months before Temple's birth. Dayton made the boys honorary policemen, and they wore their badges throughout the remainder of the trip. At a Wheeling, West Virginia, hotel they were awakened by the manager and taken onto the roof to see Halley's Comet.

Louie and Temple arrived in Washington on May 27 and visited with President William Howard Taft at the White House. The Speaker halted debate in the House long enough to introduce them to the congressmen. After they had seen Philadelphia their father met them in Trenton, New Jersey, then returned to New York while the boys continued the journey alone. They attracted huge crowds riding through downtown Manhattan. When Theodore Roosevelt arrived on June 18, Louie and Temple went out by Coast Guard cutter to meet him, then rode Sam Bass and Wylie Haynes in his welcoming parade, which drew a million spectators.

Louie wanted to return home by car, so his father bought a Brush for the boys and a Maxwell for himself. Louie drove the Brush all the way to Oklahoma while a mechanic chauffered Jack Abernathy; Louie had practiced driving on Broadway in New York City until his father was convinced that he could handle the car. The roads in the east were very poor, and west of Chicago there was no paving. The Brush had a brake but no clutch, and the gearshift was outside the car. The seat had been altered so Louie could reach the brake pedal. The 2,500-mile trip home required sixteen days and substantially wore out the cars. The horses were shipped to Oklahoma by rail.

A few months later the Brush company invited Louie and Temple to an automobile show in New York City. There some promoters hired them to stage a Democrat-Republican race to Washington; Louie rode a Republican elephant and Temple a Democrat donkey. The elephant scared horses and caused some runaways, and when his feet got sore it was necessary to stop the race in Philadelphia. The promoters then offered Louie and Temple $10,000 if they could ride horseback from one coast to the other in 60 days. They accepted the challenge, which included the condition that they eat and sleep outdoors throughout the 3,600-mile journey.

After spending a few days with Theodore Roosevelt, they left Coney Island on August 1, 1911. Ten thousand well-wishers saw them off as they started west. Louie was eleven and Temple was seven. They took a skillet and some bacon, and their father rode part of the way with them. From New York City their route was through Albany, Buffalo, Erie, Toledo, and Cleveland. While camped outside Chicago a cold rain began. Louie said:

> We like to have froze to death. So we saddled up the horses and rode for Chicago. And I'm telling you we were freezing. My brother said, "Let's go to some place that's not so cold." We came to a saloon, tied our horses, and went in. They didn't want to let us in, thought we were runaways, but we were great friends before we left. Then the next day we rode on into Chicago and it was the hottest day I ever saw. It was August and I thought we were going to get sunstroke with the heat coming off those paved streets.

Temple and Louie Abernathy rode alone from Oklahoma to New York City in 1910 to greet Theodore Roosevelt as he returned from an African big game hunt.

They passed through Des Moines and Omaha. Near Cheyenne, Wyoming, Louie's horse, the sixteen-year-old Sam Bass, died; Theodore Roosevelt had admired his stamina and intelligence when Jack Abernathy used him to hunt wolves. Sam Bass had gotten into an alfalfa field, ate too much, drank too much, and foundered. The boys were tiring as they reached Reno and crossed the mountains into California, but their spirits rose as they got to Sacramento. They rode into the Pacific Ocean at San Francisco's Golden Gate Park on the sixty-second day.

Louie was a World War I flying cadet and graduated from the law school of the University of Oklahoma in 1922. He has served as an Assistant District Attorney and Wichita County Attorney during his more than 50 years of law practice in Texas. Temple attended Hardin-Simmons University, spent most of his life in the oil business in Houston, and lives in Teague now. Jack Abernathy died in 1941, at the age of 65, in Long Beach, California, and was buried at Wichita Falls.

—*Oklahoma Historical Society*

Temple and Louie Abernathy on a typical 1910 road returning from New York City to Oklahoma City.

Temple and Louie Abernathy drove a one-cylinder Brush from New York to Oklahoma City.

This letter from Theodore Roosevelt cautions Jack Abernathy against participating in public exihibitions of wolf catching while he remains the United States Marshal for Oklahoma.

Charles Post Changed the Eating Habits of a Nation

Charles W. Post, born in Springfield, Illinois, in 1854, attended college and became a farm machinery salesman. After suffering a nervous breakdown he came to Fort Worth in September, 1886. He helped develop the Sylvania Addition and lived on a 200-acre ranch which is now in Forest Park. In late 1890 his health broke again, and he was taken to Battle Creek, Michigan, for treatment.

The Battle Creek sanitarium was operated by Seventh Day Adventists, who abstained from tobacco, alcohol, tea, coffee, spices, and meat. The superintendent, Dr. John Kellogg, and his brother and business manager, W. K. Kellogg, had devised for the patients food substitutes made from grain. As Post recovered he decided to make a coffee substitute. He had known poor West Texans who mixed chicory with roasted wheat to produce a better drink than that served by the sanitarium.

Post remained in Battle Creek, began experimenting, and developed a beverage from wheat, bran, and molasses which he called Postum. He began production in his barn, buying five gallons of molasses at a time. In January, 1895, a Grand Rapids grocer took a stock of Postum on consignment, then Post placed an advertisement in the local newspaper and brewed some Postum for the publisher and staff. Post sold only $5,000 worth of Postum that year, but using small newspaper ads to create a market he increased his 1896 sales to $265,000. Sales were $850,000 in 1898.

Post's success drew competitors, who undersold the 25¢ Postum. Because of their inroads Post decided to use the same tactics against them. He brought out Monk's Brew at 5¢, which ruined the competition. Actually Monk's Brew was simply Postum packaged under the other name; it did well against the competitors' 15¢ products, but after they were gone it would not sell. The price differential between 5¢ Monk's Brew and 25¢ Postum was too great. Post recalled the Monk's Brew, put it into Postum packages and had no difficulty selling it for a quarter.

Post's belief that a product had to have a "halo," created through advertising, made him one of the first major advertisers. He spent $60 million for advertising in the decade beginning in 1902. Because Postum sold best in the winter, Post developed a product to take up the summer production slack; Grape-Nuts, introduced in 1897, was one of the first cold cereals. Seven years later Elijah's Manna did poorly until the name was changed to Post Toasties. Post's Bran Flakes came out in 1922 and Grape-Nuts Flakes in 1932.

Post died in 1914 while building Post City, in Garza County, Texas. The Postum Cereal Company became the General Foods Corporation in 1929 after acquiring the Jell-O Company. Through the years General Foods added the makers of Swan's Down Cake Flour, Minute Tapioca, Baker's Coconut, Log Cabin Syrup, La France Satina, Maxwell House Coffee, Calumet Baking Powder, Birdseye Frozen Foods, Sanka, Yuban, Gaines dog food, and others. General Foods' sales exceeded $2.5 billion in 1973.

Charles Post, a Fort Worth real estate man, invented Postum and began General Foods.

Eddie Rickenbacker Was a Dallas Car Salesman

Edward V. Rickenbacker grew up in Columbus, Ohio. When he was thirteen his father died and he went to work, earning $3.50 for a 72-hour week. Fascinated by automobiles, at fifteen he got a job in a garage. He learned to drive by running customers' cars back and forth inside the building while his employer was away. Because he showed such promise with a small automobile manufacturer he was hired by Firestone's Columbus Buggy Company.

Firestone was doing well with its two-cylinder motor buggies when Rickenbacker demonstrated the new Firestone-Columbus touring car at the 1909 Chicago show. When the Dallas dealer, Fife and Miller, complained that their new Firestone-Columbus automobiles had broken down, Rickenbacker was sent to fix them. Of his summer arrival, 1909, in Dallas he wrote, "I had never been so hot in my life. The first thing I did . . . was to find a hotel room and take off my long underwear." He altered the engines to tolerate Texas heat, and Fife and Miller ordered more on condition that Rickenbacker would remain to help sell them.

Rickenbacker sold a motor buggy to a McLennan County physician who gave enthusiastic testimonials whenever the boy had prospects contact him. His other sure-fire technique involved taking Chalk Hill in high.

> We always made it, but one day, with a particularly heavy prospect aboard, I feared that we wouldn't. In an effort to give the buggy every chance, I made a running start and approached Chalk Hill at 30 miles an hour. The little buggy bounced and skidded on the gravel road like a skittish colt just learning to gallop. We started up the grade with my potential customer and me both leaning forward and pushing with body English. Halfway up it became all too clear to me that we were not going to make it in high gear. Quickly I slammed on the brakes and we came to a dead stop . . . . I beamed at him with a proud smile. "How do you like those brakes?" I asked. "See how they hold us tight, right here on Chalk Hill."
>
> He smiled back . . . "Holy gee, that's great!" He bought the car that afternoon, for cash.

The 18-year-old Rickenbacker helped set up dealerships over the state. Seizing upon an opportunity for publicity, he offered to chauffeur William Jennings Bryan during his Abilene visit. "Naturally there was a parade in his honor, and thousands of people from miles around saw the great William Jennings Bryan in the back seat. The picture was on the front page of the local paper." After a year he returned home, five inches taller; his mother said, "My, they grow them big in Texas."

Rickenbacker became a successful racing driver, competing against Louis Chevrolet and Barney Oldfield. In World War I he went overseas with Pershing's first American troops. He was General Billy Mitchell's driver until, at the age of 27, he entered the air service. He became the leading American ace, downing 26 enemy airplanes, and won the Congressional Medal of Honor.

Teenage car salesman Edward V. Rickenbacker, later America's leading World War I ace, drove William Jennings Bryan around Abilene, Texas.

Gus Noyes Raised a Memorial to His Son

In April, 1917, the sculptor Pompeo Coppini returned to Texas to talk to rancher Gus Noyes, whose son had been killed in an accident a few weeks earlier. Wanting to erect a statue of the boy, Noyes had first approached Waldine Tauch, who believed the work required Coppini's talents. Coppini took a train from Chicago to Melvin, Menard County, hoping to get the commission. His finances were somewhat strained, and Gus Noyes was said to be a very wealthy man.

The sculptor, dismayed when he saw the Noyes ranch, wrote:

As I looked at the simple way those people were living, the poor clothes they were all wearing, the scanty furnishings of a very poor people's home, and the unshaved, sad-looking face of Mr. Noyes, I became almost frightened that I might have been misled . . . . I was scared to talk, as I hated to show what was passing in my mind, and the tall, square-shouldered (but slightly bent), big-boned, old man sat by the fireside, with no fire in it, gazing as if there was a flame, and saying nothing and asking me no questions.

Coppini spent the night in the son's bedroom but could not sleep. Early the next morning he wandered around the ranch and talked to one of the hands about the death; Charles Noyes, 21 years old, and some of the hands were separating weaning calves from the cows when a calf broke away. His horse ran into the calf and fell with him, breaking Noyes' neck. He died in the Brady hospital that night. Coppini very much wanted to do the statue, but still worried about money he asked, "Is this Mr. Noyes really wealthy?" The cowboy answered, "One of the richest men in this part of the country, and one of the smartest, too." Somewhat relieved Coppini was not certain Noyes realized how expensive a piece of sculpture might be. He decided to set his price as low as possible in order to get the commission.

Gus Noyes drove Coppini to the pasture where the accident occurred and said, as he wept, "Here is where I want to place the monument to my son, Charlie." That afternoon the sculptor studied the few snapshots that had been taken of Charles Noyes and saw the iron-grey horse he had been riding. Then Coppini made some sketches of the work; instead of a mounted equestrian statue he proposed that Charles Noyes, who was six feet four inches tall, be represented standing by the horse. Gus Noyes approved. After supper, as they sat together in silence, the old rancher, staring into the unlighted fireplace, asked, "Well, Mr. Coppini, what is the best you can do as a price?"

The sculptor had thought that $25,000 was the least he could afford to accept, but his desire to do the piece got the better of him. He answered, "$18,000 complete and erected under my supervision."

Noyes said, "O. K., it is a deal, I thought it would cost me double that amount."

Coppini had Charles Noyes' hat, boots, spurs, saddle, and bridle shipped to his Chicago studio and began an intensive study of horses in preparation for the work. Because of the war anthracite coal was not available in Chicago that winter. Coppini was using bituminous coal—which was hard to keep burning—to heat his studio.

The Charles Noyes statue, intended for the Noyes ranch, was erected in Ballinger.

One evening during a blizzard Coppini was worried that the studio fire might go out and permit the Noyes horse, which had been done in clay, to freeze. He made his way through a blinding snowstorm to the studio; it took almost three hours to walk two miles. The fire was out, and the clay horse, once the room was warm again, "crumbled like flour."

Coppini had to start all over, but in July, 1918, he asked Mr. and Mrs. Noyes and their daughter to come to Chicago to see the memorial group. The sculptor was uneasy about the son's likeness; he had been working from the only photographs ever made of Charles Noyes, three small snapshots of very poor quality. Coppini made a few changes suggested by the family, and then Gus Noyes said, "Please do not touch it any more, as it is my Charlie now."

Coppini had the statue cast in bronze and got ready to bring it to Texas. In the meantime Gus Noyes, who had been unable to endure the ranch after the loss of his son, had sold out and moved to Florida. He had arranged for the piece to be placed on the courthouse square in Ballinger, where his son had finished high school. The statue of Charles Noyes and his horse were unveiled October 25, 1919. Its base consisted of three pieces of granite weighing some 35 tons. Coppini attended the unveiling, but Gus Noyes could not bear to be there.

Pompeo Coppini made an extensive study of horses in preparation for the Charles Noyes statue.

John Pershing Came to Mexia

Ever since the 1894 Corsicana strike Mexia residents had believed there was oil beneath their town, too. In 1912 local men drilled a shallow well which produced gas in commercial quantities, and within months some forty wells were furnishing gas to Mexia, Groesbeck, Waco, and Corsicana. The Mexia Oil and Gas Company contracted with John A. Sheppard to drill a deeper well to the oil which they believed lay below the gas. Sheppard began a test well in 1919, then moved to another location west of town. He sold half his contract to Col. A. E. Humphreys, who brought in Rogers No. 1 at 3,065 feet on November 19, 1920. The well was only a fifty-barrel producer but caused Humphreys to buy the Mexia company's leases. In May, 1921, when the third well was a 3,000-barrel gusher, the Mexia boom began.

Two gushers came in on the same August day, one flowing 18,000 barrels a day and the other yielding 24,000 barrels. Humble, Gulf, Texaco, and other major oil producers fought for leases, causing values to rise enormously; a $25 lease sold for $12,500. Derricks rose while storage and transport facilities were built. By December petroleum loading racks extended 22 miles along the railroad tracks and 40,000 tank cars were carrying Mexia crude.

Mexia's population grew from 4,000 to 40,000. The first to answer the boom lived in tents or cars or lodged six to the room in private residences. By the end of 1921 three hotels had been built, forty rooming houses were opened, and the Commercial Hotel had added fifty rooms. Railroad employees building new facilities slept in converted baggage cars. The water system was overtaxed; water, cut off each evening so that the standpipe could fill, was turned on at 6 a.m. and was gone by 9 o'clock. During the day boys carrying buckets sold drinking water by the dipperful. Those unable to get into the over-crowded cafes lived on pecans at 10¢ per handful; street vendors called, "I crack 'em and you eat 'em." The usual vice problem developed, and rangers and the national guard were sent in.

The local newspaper wanted the town's name changed to "Humphreys." The colonel's buildings were painted Confederate grey, and his derricks displayed a large "H." When Humphreys completed the first paved road in Limestone County—which connected his home with the Groesbeck highway—he named it "Pershing Way." General of the Armies John J. Pershing dedicated the road on January 6, 1922, and visitors came by special train from Dallas and Fort Worth to hear his speech.

In February, 1922, the Mexia field attained peak production, 194,205 barrels from 182 wells. More wells were drilled, but the output declined. Mexia, briefly the tenth largest city in Texas, had only 10,126 residents by November. Humphreys sold out to the Pure Oil Company and moved away the next year. By 1949 Mexia had yielded more than a million barrels of oil. Some production continues at Mexia, now a city of some 6,000.

The first paved road in Limestone County was named for General of the Armies John J. Pershing, who came to Mexia for the dedication. Colonel A. E. Humphreys stands right behind Pershing as the General breaks ground for the road.

The Mobley Was Hilton's First Hotel

Conrad Hilton, the youngest member of New Mexico's first legislature, was discharged from the Army in 1919 and came to Wichita Falls hoping to buy a bank in one of the oil boom towns. He wrote: "The first thing we saw was a town roaring like a blast furnace. It was hard to get meals, next to impossible to get beds, and inconceivable that a man could think of buying a bank." Having no luck in Breckenridge, he tried Cisco, near the Ranger field, but was unable to buy any of the five banks.

Hilton tried to get a room at Cisco's two-story, red-brick Mobley Hotel, where men seeking lodging crowded the lobby "like sardines clamoring to get into the can." H. L. Mobley, renting each room three times a day, told Hilton to "come back in eight hours when we turn this lot loose." Mobley was anxious to get into the oil business, so Hilton, 31 years old, paid $40,000 for the hotel, which he called, "a cross between a flophouse and a gold mine."

Hilton began learning the hotel business, sleeping in a chair to free bed space. He realized that:

> For us the profit was in beds. There were plenty of hash houses in Cisco to cater to the undemanding palates of our guests. I ordered in carpenters to close the dining room and split it with partitions, just space enough for a bed and a dresser. Then I had the main desk cut in half and a news and tobacco stand installed.

Hilton dreamed of a chain of Texas hotels; his second hotel was the 68-room Melba, in Fort Worth. The third was the Waldorf, in Dallas, a six-story building which had "150 rooms with a sprinkling of baths and a fifty-room annex, no baths at all." After refurbishing the Waldorf, Hilton's earnings from the three hotels was $6,000 a month. Business was good, and desk clerks were told to say, "I'm sorry that we haven't a single, but I could let you have a room with three other gentlemen."

In 1925 he built the Dallas Hilton at Main and Harwood. By October, 1929, Hilton had hotels operating or under construction in Abilene, Waco, Dallas, Marlin, Plainview, San Angelo, Lubbock, and El Paso. He lost them all after the crash. Once when he was broke and owed half a million dollars, a bellboy, Eddie Fowler, lent him $300.

In the middle thirties Hilton was able to buy back some of his hotels. Many of the finest hotels had been taken over by mortgage holders who could not operate them and would sell cheaply. In 1937, Hilton paid $275,000 for San Francisco's Sir Francis Drake, which had originally cost $4 million; it was his first hotel outside of Texas. In the next few years he bought the Stevens, in Chicago, then the largest hotel in the world, the Roosevelt and Hotel Plaza, in New York, Chicago's Palmer House, and the Mayflower, in Washington. In 1949 Hilton bought the Waldorf Astoria and five years later he paid $111 million for the Statler hotels.

174

The Mobley Hotel, in Cisco, was to be Conrad Hilton's first in a string of Texas hotels.

The Malakoff Heads Were Found in Henderson County

On November 2, 1929, Cuban-born Indelicio Morgado and his helpers were digging gravel near Cedar Creek in western Henderson County when, at a depth of 16 feet, they found an interesting stone. The gravel in the pit had been teacup-size or smaller, so they were somewhat surprised to find this rounded boulder on the clay bottom. As Morgado turned over the stone he noticed that there were markings; it was a representation of the human head. Indelicio and his brother, Teo Morgado, had contracted with Texas Clay Products, of Malakoff, to dig gravel on Judge W. R. Bishop's farm. Since it was Saturday and almost noon, the boulder was not removed from the pit until Monday, which was just as well; it had lain undisturbed for several thousand years. Another weekend would not matter.

As the stone was loaded into a dump truck by hoist it was dropped, and a piece was broken off. Teo Morgado put the head beside him in the seat to keep it from further damage, and after dumping the gravel at the Malakoff construction site, he set the stone at one end, as if it were a tombstone. It attracted the attention of T. A. Bartlett, the president of Texas Clay Products Company—who later gave the stone to the Texas Memorial Museum—and V. C. Doctorman, a mining engineer. Doctorman wrote to Dr. E. H. Sellards, the director of the museum at Austin, on November 9, 1929:

> In a gravel pit about four and a half miles west of Malakoff, where some workmen were excavating, was found a roughly carved stone which upon further investigation proved to be shaped very much like a human skull. Diamond-shaped openings have been carved to represent the eyes and an attempt has been made to properly represent the ears, nose and mouth.

Sellards came to Henderson County on November 26. He described the image as follows:

> The excavation for the right eye is about 53 mm. long by 20 wide and 10 deep. That for the left eye is about 50 mm. long by 25 wide and scarcely as deep as that for the right eye. The eyebrows are represented by lines which, however, are not entirely alike, that of the right eye being more carefully carved. The markings for the left eye are somewhat better preserved and less dulled by oxidation than are those of the right eye. The nose, which is low and broad, is brought out in relief by slight excavation at either side. The excavation for the mouth is 120 mm. from side to side, 35 mm. across at the widest part, and 8 or 10 mm. in depth. The mouth opening is not symmetrical, the right half being larger, deeper, and seemingly more nicely finished than the left half. Teeth are represented at the lower side of the mouth by sloping excavations made, apparently, with a boring implement. Six such bore holes seem to represent lower teeth. The smaller bore holes may have been intended to represent upper teeth, although the resemblance is less perfect. The ears are carved in relief. The left is the better preserved and projects as much as 8 mm. from the head. As carved, the ear is 70 mm. long by 35 wide. The chin is set off by a lightly excavated line seemingly representing a double chin.

176

In a gravel pit beneath present Cedar Creek Lake workmen found the first of the Malakoff heads.

The sandstone was decayed to such a degree that 16.9 grams sloughed off between December 18 and January 4, 1930, when the surface was treated with gum arabic to halt the disintegration. The weight of the stone was 98⅜ pounds; it was 16 inches long and 14 inches wide.

In September, 1935, a second head was found on the Bishop farm about a thousand feet west of the first excavation. Joe Gunnels found it near the botton of a gravel deposit. The stone, about 15 inches long and weighing 63 ¼ pounds, was treated with gum arabic to stop the deterioration caused by exposure to the air. It is in the possession of Mrs. Lynn Sanders of Corsicana.

The third carved stone was discovered in November, 1939, at a depth of 22 feet, in the gravel pit where the first one was found. The stone weighed 135 pounds and may have been intended to represent an animal or a man. The searchers, funded by the University of Texas and the Works Progress Administration, photographed the stone before moving it.

As to the age of these carvings, they were made before the ancient Trinity River began covering them with gravel, well before the close of the Pleistocene period. In the gravel pits where the images were found were discovered fossils of the extinct elephant, horse, camel, and ground sloth. The Malakoff heads are many thousands of years old, or as Sellards wrote: "The age in years is that represented by the lowering of the flood plain of the (Trinity) river sixty or seventy feet through three successive stages, during each of which a broad river valley was formed."

The site is now covered by Cedar Creek Lake and the two heads not privately owned are on display in the Texas Memorial Museum at Austin.

The first Malakoff head was found by Teo and Indelicio Morgado near Trinidad, Texas. The site is now covered by Cedar Creek Lake.

The third Malakoff head was discovered by a group funded by the WPA and the University of Texas.

These carved stones were found in gravel pits under present Cedar Creek Lake.

Wiley Post Flew Around the World Alone

Wiley Hardeman Post was born in Van Zandt County, Texas, November 22, 1898. In 1902 his family moved to a farm near Abilene, where they remained five years before going to Oklahoma. From the time Post saw his first airplane at the 1913 county fair in Lawton he dreamed of engines and flight. He attended a Kansas City automotive school and was studying radio in the Student Army Training Corps when World War I ended. While working in the oil fields he paid $25 for an airplane ride. In 1924 he went to see Burrell Tibbs' "Texas Top-notch Fliers" at Wewoka; because Tibbs' parachute jumper was injured Post took the job. He made 99 jumps in the next two years while learning to fly. For his solo flight he posted a $200 deposit to cover the damage he might do to Sam Bartel's $150 airplane.

In 1926 Post injured an eye while roughnecking in the oil fields; with his $1698.25 workman's compensation award he bought a $200 airplane and spent $340 for repairs. The injured eye had to be removed, which would cause difficulty when he had to get a pilot's license.

In 1927 Post and Mae Laine, of Sweetwater, Texas, eloped in a Curtiss Canuck. The engine failed near Graham, Oklahoma; they found a preacher and were married, but Post had no money to repair the damaged airplane. J. Bart Scott bought the plane, repaired it, and hired Post to barnstorm for him. Then F. C. Hall and another oil man, who intended to use an airplane in their business, hired Post. Post's physical defect was waived and he was licensed as an air transport pilot. Hall bought a Lockheed Vega, which he named for his daughter, Winnie Mae Fain. After the stock market crash Hall sold the *Winnie Mae*, but the new owner let Post fly her as escort for the 1929 women's air race in which Amelia Earhart placed third.

Post flew Hall's second *Winnie Mae* in the 1930 National Air Races, which he won; Art Goebel took second place in the first *Winnie Mae*. Post then began to plan a flight around the world. Two Army Air Service teams had flown Douglas biplanes around the world in 1924. Their trip took nearly six months. The *Graf Zepplin* had circumnavigated the globe in 21 days in August, 1929. Post's flight would be the third in history.

After persuading Australian-born Harold Gatty to be his navigator, Post began modifying the *Winnie Mae* while government officials got permission for him to fly over Russia. From Roosevelt Field, Lindbergh's 1927 point of departure, they took off on Tuesday, June 23, 1931, at 4:55 p.m. Stopping at Harbour Grace, Newfoundland; Liverpool, England; Hanover and Berlin, Germany; Moscow, Novo-Sibirsk, Irktusk, Blagoveshchensk, and Khabarovsk, in Russia; Solomon and Fairbanks, Alaska, Edmonton, Canada; and Cleveland, Ohio, they landed at New York City on July 1 at 8:47 p.m. They had covered 15,474 miles in 8 days, 15 hours, and 51 minutes. New York gave them a ticker tape parade, President Herbert Hoover welcomed them to the White House, and Will Rogers hosted a banquet in their honor at Claremore, Oklahoma.

Wiley Post twice flew the *Winnie Mae* around the world.

Wiley Post bought the *Winnie Mae* from Hall and began planning a solo flight in 1933. The depression made financing difficult. Tom Braniff and three others pledged their salaries to cover repairs to the *Winnie Mae*, and 41 Oklahoma citizens contributed to finance the flight.

When Jimmy Mattern, of San Angelo, began his solo attempt on June 3, Post was still not ready to leave. Mattern crashed in Siberia twelve days later. Post left from Floyd Bennett Field, New York City, at 5:10 a.m. on July 15, 1933, making the first non-stop flight to Germany in spite of trouble with his automatic pilot. From Berlin he stopped at Koenigsberg, Germany, then Novo-Sibirsk, Irkutsk, Rukhlovo, and Khabarovsk in Russia. On the way to Fairbanks, Alaska, he got lost and landed at Flat, Alaska, where the *Winnie Mae* skidded into a ditch and bent the propeller. Pacific Airways employees repaired the plane while Post slept and showed him the way to Fairbanks. From Fairbanks he flew to Edmonton, Canada. On the 2,044 mile leg to New York he used the automatic pilot, holding a wrench, which was tied to his finger by a string, so that if he fell asleep the falling wrench would wake him. Some 50,000 New Yorkers met him at Floyd Bennett Field on July 23. His time was 7 days, 18 hours and 49½ minutes and broke his own record by 21 hours. He was the first to fly around the world twice, and the first to do it alone. Post's time record stood until Texan Howard Hughes, with a four-man crew, circled the world in 3 days, 19 hours, and 8 minutes, in 1938.

Probably Post's most important contribution was his work in stratospheric flight. Post had the B. F. Goodrich Company make a rubberized suit, which he wore at 40,000 feet on September 5, 1934, in the first such flight ever made. His pressurized suit was the foundation for systems which would later permit Americans to walk on the moon. After proving the desirability and practicability of stratospheric travel, the *Winnie Mae* was worn out. Congressman Josh Lee, of Oklahoma, introduced a resolution permitting the Smithsonian to buy the *Winnie Mae*.

After retiring the *Winnie Mae*, Post bought what he called an Explorer-Orion. A Lockheed Orion had been wrecked, as had a Lockheed Explorer. The Explorer wings were fitted to the Orion fuselage. Post intended to fly into Siberia, and Will Rogers decided to go along to gather material for his newspaper column. Rogers was to pay the expenses. When the pontoons Post wanted were not available in Seattle he bought larger ones, which made the airplane nose heavy. Neither was willing to wait for proper pontoons; Post believed Rogers' weight in the back of the plane would correct the nose problem.

They bought a case of chili in Seattle and left at 9:20 a.m., August 6, 1935. They stopped at Juneau, Alaska, then went on to Dawson and Fairbanks. Rogers wanted to see Charlie Brower, a trader and whaler at Point Barrow, 300 miles inside the Arctic Circle and 500 miles from Fairbanks. Landing on a lagoon about 16 miles from Barrow, Post asked Eskimos for directions and had something to eat. As they took off, the engine quit. The plane crashed, killing Will Rogers and Wiley Post at approximately 8:18 p.m., August 15, 1935. Post was buried at Edmond, Oklahoma, after lying in state at the Oklahoma capitol. With the $25,000 Congress appropriated for the *Winnie Mae*, Mrs. Post bought a home near Ralls, Texas.

—*B. F. Goodrich Company*

Wiley Post devised a pressure suit for high altitude flight to prove his theory that higher speeds were possible in the stratosphere.

A Generation Died at New London

New London resulted from C. M. Joiner's East Texas oil strike in 1930. Situated near 40-year-old London, in Rusk County, New London had 600 residents within weeks of its founding. It was a place to live and a trading center for oil field workers. The New London Consolidated School District claimed to be the nation's wealthiest. Located in the greatest oil field in the world, there were seven producing wells on its property. The fireproof New London School, completed in 1932, had cost some $300,000; it was 250 feet long by 146 feet wide, built of steel frame, hollow tile, and brick. Constructed in the shape of an "E", it was a one-story structure except for the auditorium, in the middle, and portions of the two wings, which were two-story. The school served an area of some 30 square miles.

Thursday afternoon, March 18, 1937, was bright and warm in New London By 3:20 o'clock the primary grades had been dismissed; the remaining 600 students would be free in another ten minutes. The Parent-Teacher Association was meeting in the gymnasium nearby. Some of the younger children played in the schoolyard while waiting for buses or older brothers and sisters. Then, without warning, the New London School exploded.

Gas collected beneath the building was apparently ignited when a shop teacher turned on a sanding machine. The gas shot the floor upward, throwing bricks 200 feet into the air, and blew the walls outward. Then the roof caved in. Within an instant all that remained of the school was part of the north wing and portions of the auditorium and south wing walls. The rest was only a cloud of dust and flying debris.

Thirteen teachers and visitors and 280 students died in the catastrophe. Approximately 85 children were injured. The death count would have been greater had the school been located anywhere else, for there would not have been available so much heavy equipment and so many skilled operators. Within minutes hundreds of oil field workers were there with trucks and cranes removing debris to free those trapped beneath the wreckage. Beginning with the dead and injured children who had been playing outside and those blown through the windows, the rescuers worked toward the school, clearing the area as they went to be certain no child remained beneath the debris. Meanwhile the highways were filled with cars and trucks taking the injured to hospitals in other towns and bringing parents and workers to the school. Sightseers' automobiles clogged the roads. By early evening 214 bodies had been recovered; the principal of the school feared that the deaths would number 500.

President Franklin Roosevelt urged the Red Cross and government agencies to render all possible assistance. Governor James V. Allred declared martial law, sent in the national guard, and ordered a military court of inquiry to determine the cause of the blast. Medical supplies were sent from all over the state, and physicians, nurses, and embalmers rushed to New London. The national guard troops numbered about 200 and came from Tyler, Longview, and Marshall. The martial law declaration subordinated civil authorities to the military; thousands of sightseers got in the way of those doing relief work, and New London's officers were unable

This school took the place of the one destroyed in the New London explosion.

to handle them. The governor asked those without business in New London to stay away and warned that the curious would be turned back; all available highway patrol officers had been sent to Rusk County.

That night the schoolyard was illuminated by fires from gas pipes jutting 30 feet into the air and floodlights from the football field. Some 5,000 people formed a ring in the center of which oil field roughnecks searched the rubble. Two thousand men in long lines passed debris, hand to hand, out to the edge of the clearing. School books were gathered in peach baskets. The gymnasium and almost every church and public building in the area became morgues. Parents passed along rows of bodies trying to find their children. Some were identified by fingerprints; the Department of Public Safety had taken prints of many of the students at the 1936 Texas Centennial as part of a drive to record a million fingerprints. An information station was opened in the Overton City Hall to list the dead and injured.

The search was concluded on March 19; a pouring rain in the last hours made the work more difficult. Trucks could not get traction in the muddy ground and cables slipped as wreckage was lifted. It was Texas' worst disaster since the Galveston flood. Funerals for almost 100 children were held on March 20 at London, Overton, Kilgore, Tyler, Henderson, Marshall, and Shreveport. The highway patrol complained that sightseers were impeding traffic. The next day Chief L. C. Phares announced: "There will be nearly 200 funerals tomorrow. Isn't it hard enough for those people to bear up under this terrific loss without causing them further trouble in making decent burial difficult or impossible?" At one time the Reverend John Welch of Pleasant Hill Methodist Church was preaching a funeral service over eight coffins, while across the road at the cemetery graveside services were being held for five more.

The military court of inquiry adjourned on March 22. Testimony was that the addition of a malodorant to the gas would have prevented the catastrophe. A fifteen-year-old student testified that the explosion occurred right after his manual training teacher threw a light switch; however, an expert testified that the blast could have been triggered by a leak in any of the school's 72 radiators.

Classes were resumed on March 29, after the school board decided not to send the children to another town. There was a light snow and raw wind as 287 students met in the gymnasium, which was not heated because of fear of escaping gas. Substitutes filled in for dead teachers. The roll calls provided the first really accurate count of those who died. The fifth and sixth grades were the most heavily hit. More than half of some 90 graduating seniors were killed in the explosion. Many families lost more than one child; one lost four. The youngest victim, below school age, had been waiting with his mother for school to let out and had run inside the building just before the explosion.

The present $350,000 school building and the marble memorial were erected in 1938. Every known safety feature was built into the new school.

A monument commemorates the 298 victims of the New London disaster.

189

Texans Tried to Steal Moses Austin's Bones

Connecticut-born Moses Austin lived in Pennsylvania and Virginia prior to obtaining 6,085 acres in Missouri—which was then Spanish territory—in 1797. He mined and smelted lead and founded Potosi, Missouri's second oldest city. After sustaining heavy financial losses in the failure of the Bank of St. Louis, Austin came to San Antonio seeking permission to settle colonists in Spanish Texas. Through the intervention of an old friend, the Baron de Bastrop, Austin's request was later granted. Austin became ill on his journey home; deserted and robbed by traveling companions, he and his servant, Richmond, suffered from exposure and starvation. He died June 10, 1821, at Far Blue in St. Francois County, Missouri. Later his body was moved to the Presbyterian and Masonic Cemetery at Potosi, the first transaction involving Austin's mortal remains and certainly the most orderly and productive one.

Stephen F. Austin accepted the Texas grant and spent his life fulfilling his father's dream. He died as a young man soon after Texas became a republic, in December, 1836. Later Austin was re-interred in the State Cemetery; eventually some Texans decided Moses Austin should be buried beside his son in the city which bore their name.

The first notoriety involving Moses Austin's grave grew out of a rumor that the body had become petrified. Some of the curious invaded the grave and found the rumor false. Then a wild cherry tree took root on the grave, supposedly sprung from a cherry stone in Austin's pocket. In 1904 the *Potosi Journal* reported that the tree had been cut down a few years earlier; old timers had made walking canes of the cherry wood, and the stump, nearly three feet in diameter, was displayed at St. Louis' Louisiana Purchase Exposition in 1904.

The most exciting episode involving the grave occurred in 1938. On April 21, the *St. Louis Post-Dispatch* reported that, "An attempt to remove the bones of Moses Austin, founder of Potosi, who died in 1821, from its grave in Presbyterian and Masonic Cemetery, here, for reburial in Texas was formally halted by an order issued by the Potosi City Council in special session this morning." Major W. L. Edmonds, summoned by sharp-eyed Potosi residents, had hurried to the cemetery and discovered an Austin, Texas, undertaker and some helpers digging into the 117-year-old grave. The undertaker exhibited documents signed by Austin's descendants authorizing the removal, but the Missourians were not satisfied.

The Missouri State Historical Society commended the mayor for his stand. The *Post-Dispatch* reported on April 26:

> Mayor Edmonds, in view of statements that the people of Texas do not think Missouri has properly taken care of the grave of Austin, founder of Potosi, has issued an appeal to interested Missourians for donations for the purpose of placing a suitable monument at the grave and a granite fence to enclose it. He has asked that the contributions be sent to him.

The historical society president was reminded of a like event in Missouri's past, "You will perhaps remember that a number of years ago the bodies of Daniel Boone and his wife were removed to Kentucky under somewhat similar circumstances."

Texans tried to remove the remains of Moses Austin from this tomb at Potosi, Washington County, Missouri.

The undertaker, halted in his task on Wednesday, repaired the vault at his own expense. While indignation still burned in Potosi breasts, on Saturday a Texan told the press he understood that the Austin grave was poorly maintained, a circumstance which "reflected somewhat on Texas." The outraged Potosi mayor replied, "Who do they think they are? It was in excellent condition until their workmen tore out the side of the vault."

In the next few weeks a St. Louis attorney, a descendant of Moses Austin, offered his services to oppose the Texas claim. The grave had, for years, been neglected. On the four-foot tombstone was inscribed only Austin's name and an erroneous date of death. The Moses Austin Memorial Society was formed at Potosi and a drive begun to raise a suitable marker. Texas Governor James V. Allred apologized for the undertaker's precipitate actions—recalling the fine relationship that had always been maintained with Missouri—and offered to donate $1,000 for a monument at Potosi if Austin's remains were sent to Texas. Allred would dedicate the Potosi memorial, and Austin would be buried in the State Cemetery beneath a $10,000 monument.

For a decade Moses Austin was left in peace, but in January, 1949, the Potosi Lions Club proposed that Texas give $50,000 for a new Potosi city hall in return for Austin's bones. The *St. Louis Post-Dispatch* recalled that the 1941 Missouri legislature had authorized the raising of funds for an appropriate memorial at Potosi.

> In recent years, however, travelers have been a bit puzzled as to why Potosi resented Texas' efforts to snatch away Moses Austin's bones. There is no memorial; no sign is visible in the town's streets to tell who Moses Austin was, or where he is buried. The old-timers know, however; if you ask them they will show you the old and neglected Presbyterian churchyard, and they will direct you through a wilderness of brush and debris to a tomb all but obscured by weeds.

The mayor, upset by this new controversy, said, in the *Potosi Independent-Journal*, "I will state that the Lions' Club or any other club or organization does not have authority to make any plans or arrangements or negotiations with anyone regarding the removal of the bones of our beloved Moses Austin, founder of our city." The *Journal* also printed a Denton, Texas, letter charging that Austin committed an unpardonable sin in being "caught dead in Missouri" and deserved to stay there.

In 1963, Frank X. Tolbert, of the *Dallas News*, revived the quarrel. Potosi Mayor Clyde Loomis stated:

> What you bone-hunting Texans don't seem to realize is that Moses Austin was the founder of Potosi .... What if a bunch of Missourians came into Dallas and demanded the bones of the man who founded your city? I think you'd get angry!

President Truman failed to carry Potosi after a 1948 speech in which he said Texas should have the bones. In 1968 it was rumored that Texans would give $100,000 for a Moses Austin Memorial Park and Swimming Pool. The *Journal* believed an offer would be declined although nothing had been done about a memorial. In 1971 the old Presbyterian Church in the cemetery was made into a museum, and a gas light was installed at Moses Austin's grave.

Moses Austin's statue, done by Waldine Tauch, the student of Pompeo Coppini, stands across the street from the Governor's Palace in San Antonio.

Claudia Taylor Became the First Lady

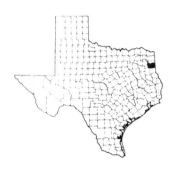

Coming to Texas from Alabama, Thomas Jefferson Taylor, II, opened a store at Karnack. He married Minnie Lee Patillo and prospered as a merchant, farmer, cattle raiser, ginner, and whatever else he chose to do. He bought an old house made of bricks which had been burned by slaves.

By the time Claudia Alta Taylor was born there on December 22, 1912, the brick house had been painted white; she was the third child; her two older brothers were Thomas Jefferson Taylor, III, and Antonio J. Taylor. Her nursemaid had exclaimed, "She's as purty as a lady bird," and in time her real name was almost forgotten. Lady Bird was five years old when her mother died. Mrs. Taylor was coming up the main stairway in the brick house when the family dog ran into her, causing her to trip and fall. She died on September 14, 1918, when she was 44.

Lady Bird could read by the age of five, when she entered the one-room Fern School. Her classmates were the children of tenant farmers. At the end of one term she was the only pupil remaining; all the others in the seven grades had left as their fathers moved to other farms. Mr. Taylor owned 18,000 acres of farmland, most of it worked by tenants, but the brick house had only coal oil lamps until Lady Bird was nine years old. Of the schoolhouse she remembered that "there was a big stove in the middle of the room, and it was always one of the big boy's jobs to bring in the wood and get the stove going in the morning."

After her mother's death Lady Bird spent a great deal of time with her father. Her brothers were at boarding schools. She would go to work with her father, play in the store, and take naps on a cot upstairs. Her aunt came from Alabama to take care of her, and when Lady Bird was ready for high school she and her Aunt Effie moved to an apartment in Jefferson. As a junior she returned to Karnack and drove to and from Marshall High School, 15 miles away by dirt road; she was 14 years old. After graduation, in 1928, she and her aunt lived in Dallas, where she attended a junior college, St. Mary's Episcopal School for Girls. Afterward she entered the University of Texas. She graduated with a major in education in 1933, and stayed another year for a bachelor's degree in journalism.

As a reward for earning the second degree, her father gave Lady Bird a trip to New York and Washington. A friend had suggested that she look up Lyndon Johnson, who was the secretary of Congressman Richard Mifflin Kleberg, the grandson of the King Ranch founder. She did not contact Johnson on that vacation, but soon after returning to Austin Lady Bird was in the office of the same friend when Johnson happened by. He asked her out that evening, but she was busy. He then invited her to breakfast the following morning at the Driskill Hotel, which she accepted, and he asked her to marry him. The next day Johnson took her to meet his parents; then they went down to the King Ranch to see the congressman. As Johnson returned to Washington he took Lady Bird to Karnack so he could meet Mr. Taylor.

194

Claudia Taylor was born in this brick house at Karnack.

Marie Smith, in her book *The President's Lady*, has a fine account of the Johnson wedding and the missing license. After a few weeks Johnson came to Karnack and insisted that she marry him. She was reluctant, but Johnson had his friend, Dan Quill, the San Antonio postmaster, make arrangements for them to be married there.

Quill contacted the rector of St. Marks Episcopal Church, who agreed to perform the wedding. As the ceremony was beginning, Lady Bird asked Johnson if he had brought a ring; he had not thought of that, so he sent best man Dan Quill for one. Quill hurried to the nearest store, Sears, Roebuck. Because he did not know the size he took a tray of rings back to the church. Lady Bird sorted through them until she found one that fit; Quill returned the others and paid $2.50 for the ring, which was his wedding gift to the couple.

The Episcopal priest who married them had never seen Johnson or Lady Bird before, and they left without giving any address. After he filled out the certificate he forwarded the marriage license to the county clerk. By Texas law the county clerk records the marriage and then returns the license to the parties, but the Clerk of Bexar County did not know the Johnsons and had no address for them. As a result the license was pinned to the page where the marriage was recorded; there it remained for 25 years, Johnson assuming that the county clerk had mailed the license and he had misplaced it. Periodically, during that quarter of a century, Lady Bird would wish she had her marriage license, and Johnson would feel guilty about it. After Johnson became vice president he was in San Antonio to address a Rotary Convention and Dan Quill was present. Johnson mentioned the loss of the marriage license and asked him to have a duplicate made. When Quill called at the courthouse and a clerk started to make the copy, she found the original, and Lady Bird finally received her marriage license.

Lady Bird and Lyndon Johnson pose beside the capitol.

Nimitz Accepted the Japanese Surrender

Chester W. Nimitz, the son of Chester B. and Anna Henke Nimitz, was born February 24, 1885, across the street from Fredericksburg's Nimitz Hotel. His father died six months before his birth, but he was close to his grandfather, Captain Charles H. Nimitz, who told the boy: "The sea—like life itself—is a stern taskmaster. The best way to get along with either is to learn all you can, then do your best and don't worry—especially about things over which you have no control."

When Chester Nimitz sought entrance to West Point there was no vacancy, but his congressman offered an appointment to Annapolis; it was the reverse of Dwight Eisenhower's situation. Eisenhower had hoped to attend the Naval Academy. Of the study required for the entrance examination, Nimitz wrote:

> This meant sandwiching extra bookwork into a busy boyhood schedule. I got up at 3 a.m. and studied until 5:30, when it was time to light the stoves. School was from 9 a.m. to 4 p.m.—followed by more chores and homework until 10 p.m.

A 1905 honor graduate, Nimitz was given command of the gunboat *Panay* in the Philippines. At 22 he became skipper of an old destroyer, the USS *Decatur*, and was court-martialed for running her aground. Assigned to the new submarine service he commanded the *Plunger*, the *Snapper*, the *Narwhal*, and the *Skipjack* and was among the few Americans who understood the weapon Germany was using so effectively at the beginning of World War I. In 1926 Nimitz took charge of an experimental naval reserve officers training program at the University of California. He proved that the training provided good officers, and the plan was followed in 52 other institutions.

After the attack on Pearl Habor, Nimitz replaced Admiral Husband Kimmel as commander of the Pacific Fleet. The United States Navy had suffered its worst defeat in history. Nimitz set about restoring morale. He wrote:

> I also knew that the confidence of the American public in the U.S. Navy had to be strengthened. One way to do this, I reasoned, was to create an atmosphere of quiet determination and orderly planning . . . . I set up a pistol range just outside my office. Near my living quarters, a half mile away, I had a horseshoe court built. I spent a lot of time at both places, and often invited war correspondents to join me. I hoped they would report the confident, relaxed atmosphere, and they did.

As the enemy was pushed back Nimitz commanded two and a half million men and attained the five-star rank of Fleet Admiral. He was one of the United States representatives who signed the Japanese surrender document aboard his flagship, the USS *Missouri*, in Tokyo Bay on September 2, 1945.

After Nimitz's death on February 20, 1966, Admiral Arleigh Burke said:

> His profound knowledge of naval warfare . . . his extraordinary wisdom in determining which was the best course of action from the many courses of action which were possible . . . his unique ability to choose men who were exactly suitable for the job which they were to do . . . all contributed to the tremendous success of the United States forces in the Pacific.

In this Fredericksburg house, across the street from the Nimitz Hotel, Chester W. Nimitz was born.

Captain Charles Nimitz, the founder of the Nimitz Hotel and his grandson, Chester, posed for this photograph in Fredericksburg.

—*United States Navy*

Fleet Admiral Chester W. Nimitz accepts the surrender of the Japanese aboard the *U. S. S. Missouri* in Tokyo Bay, September 2, 1945, as General of the Army Douglas MacArthur, Fleet Admiral William T. Halsey, General Jonathan Wainwright and others look on.

Inouye Became an Honorary Texan

In 1899, a fire occurred in the Yokoyama, Japan, home of Wasaburo Inouye which destroyed two neighboring houses. The village elders decreed that Inouye pay the equivalent of $400 to the neighbors. Because the family barely earned a living, Wasaburo sent his son to the Hawaiian sugar cane fields. Asakichi Inouye, 28 years old, his wife, and four-year old son, Hyotaro, left Yokoyama on September 28, 1899. Asakichi's two younger children remained with Wasaburo. Asakichi assumed he could pay the $400 during his five year contract, for he would earn $10 a month. Actually it required 28 years to satisfy the debt. In the meantime Hyotaro got an education, married, and worked in town.

Hyotaro's son, Daniel, born September 7, 1924, was seventeen when nearby Pearl Harbor was attacked. Because of prejudice and the practical problem of their being mistaken for the enemy the Army refused to enlist Japanese-Americans; those already in were ordered to San Francisco to form the 100th Infantry Battalion. Because of protests against Army policy, in 1943 the President ordered the establishment of a Japanese-American Combat Team, to include the 442nd Infantry Regiment, for European service. The 442nd was made up of some 4,500 Japanese-Americans chosen from three times that number of volunteers; Daniel Inouye was one of the successful candidates. During their training at Camp Shelby, Mississippi, they were fascinated by snakes, never having seen any in Hawaii.

The 442nd reached Italy in June, 1944, and became one of the most decorated regiments in World War II. The casualty rate was so large that eventually some 12,000 men were required to fill the 4,500 places. Inouye was promoted to sergeant during some of the hardest fighting of the war.

In late 1944 the 442nd was attached to the 36th division, the Texas National Guard, when the First Battalion of the 141st Infantry was cut off by the Germans near Biffontaine. This was the 36th Division's "lost battalion," almost a thousand men, mostly Texans, short of ammunition, water, and medical supplies. The battalion could not fight its way out, and no one had been able to break through to it. On October 27 the 442nd began its successful rescue effort, at a cost of some 800 casualties. When the decimated regiment was relieved in mid-November, Inouye's company, with 197 men normally, had only 40 able for duty. Every member of the 442nd was made an honorary Texan.

Inouye had become a second lieutenant in early November; because he weighed only 111 pounds the examining surgeon invented another 25 pounds to meet the Army minimum. In March, 1945, the 442nd was shipped back to Italy. Expelling the Germans from Italy would hasten the surrender. On April 21, as Inouye's platoon was moving against a high ridge it was pinned down by three machine guns. Inouye got up to throw a grenade into the nearest bunker. He was hit in the stomach but lobbed the grenade, and after it exploded he shot the gun crew. The other two German guns were still firing. Inouye destroyed one with grenades, but his men were pinned down in front of the other; Inouye, flanking the Germans, was the

Senator Daniel Inouye, an honorary Texan, questions a Watergate witness as Senator Herman Talmadge, of Georgia, looks on.

only one in a position to destroy the machine gun nest. Inouye wrote:

> All the time I was shuffling my painful way up on the flank of the emplacement, and at last I was close enough to pull the pin on my last grenade. And as I drew my arm back, all in a flash of light and dark I saw him, that faceless German . . . . One instant he was standing waist-high in the bunker, and the next he was aiming a rifle grenade at my face from a range of ten yards. And even as I cocked my arm to throw, he fired and his rifle grenade smashed into my right elbow and exploded and all but tore my arm off. I looked at it, stunned and unbelieving. It dangled there by a few bloody shreds of tissue, my grenade still clenched in a fist that suddenly didn't belong to me anymore . . . . The grenade mechanism was ticking off seconds. In two, three, or four, it would go off, finishing me and the good men who were rushing up to help me. "Get back!" I screamed, and swung around to pry the grenade out of that dead fist with my left hand. Then I had it free and I turned to throw and the German was reloading his rifle. But this time I beat him. My grenade blew up in his face and I stumbled to my feet, closing on the bunker, firing my tommy gun left-handed, the useless right arm slapping red and wet against my side . . . . It was almost over. But some last German, in his terminal instant of life squeezed off a final burst from the machine gun and a bullet caught me in the right leg and threw me to the ground and I rolled over and over down the hill.

Nine days later the war was over in Italy, and Germany surrendered the next week. Inouye lost his right arm. He received the Distinguished Service Cross and three Purple Hearts. After graduating from the University of Hawaii, he took his law degree at George Washington University and practiced law in Hawaii. Inouye became Hawaii's first congressman and was elected to the Senate in 1963, the first Japanese-American to serve in that body. As an honorary Texan Inouye felt particularly close to Lyndon Johnson and Sam Rayburn; he flew from Honolulu to attend the Speaker's funeral in Bonham.

In 1960, while Congressman Inouye was attending an international conference in Tokyo, the American ambassador suggested he see Yokoyama, something Inouye had always wanted to do. He wrote of the visit: "Here where I now stood, and everywhere along this long valley, uncounted generations of Inouyes had lived and worked in quiet simplicity and died and been laid to rest." Inouye was presented a samurai sword and escorted to the ancestral home. His uncle greeted him and then took him to the burial ground of his ancestors. Inouye stood at the graves, "lost in thoughts of what might have happened to me if it had not been for a fire on a still night so long ago."

Inouye noted that the people of Yokoyama were impressed by him, but not so much because he was a congressman. Of more importance, he had been an Army officer and his father had sent his four children to college. But most of all he was admired because he was the descendant of two generations of Inouyes who had labored for 28 years to pay a just debt.

Congressman Inouye and his mother greet Vice President Lyndon Johnson at Hickam
Air Force Base, Hawaii.

Lt. Daniel Inouye and his father in December, 1946.

Major Carswell Sank a Japanese Cruiser

Horace Carswell, Jr. was born July 18, 1916, in Fort Worth. He graduated from North Side High School, where he played in the Steers' backfield. After a year at A & M he enrolled at T.C.U., hoping to play football. His lack of size was a handicap, but he was a fierce competitor. Unfortunately the Horned Frogs had an abundance of talented backs such as Jimmy Lawrence and All American Sam Baugh. As a result Carswell did not play as much as he would have liked.

After graduation Carswell worked for an insurance firm, then, in 1940, he became an Army pilot. While stationed at Goodfellow Field in San Angelo he married Virginia Ede. He was a bold flier who buzzed T.C.U.'s Goode Hall and his father-in-law's Concho River camp. His mother said, "Horace did not know what fear was. He was happy-go-lucky and always a daredevil . . . ."

Just before he went overseas Carswell told his father, "I'm going because I know how to fly and I think I can give the Japanese some trouble." His son, Robert Ede Carswell, was six weeks old at the time. After his plane was shot down over the Himalayas he wrote a friend, "The Toads never quit. I found out that a man is never through until he quits . . . ." He got back to his base just in time to stop the message to his wife reporting him missing in action.

On October 16, 1944, Major Carswell was flying a seasweep mission off the China coast when he discovered a Japanese task force of six vessels, including a cruiser and a destroyer. Major Carswell took his B-24 in at 400 feet and made four runs in spite of very heavy fire. He sank the destroyer and cruiser and barely had enough gasoline to get back to his base. The citation for his Distinguished Service Cross read: "The exceptional courage, gallantry, cool judgment and skill demonstrated by Major Carswell in attacking such a large task force with his lone plane in the face of almost certain destruction reflect the highest credit upon himself . . . ."

Eleven days later Major Carswell made a low-level attack on a Japanese convoy in the South China Sea, sank one ship, and damaged another badly, but two of his Liberator bomber's four engines were knocked out. On the way back to his base the other engines began to fail. Major Carswell ordered the crew to bail out, but the bombardier, Lt. Walter W. Hillier, of Chicago, reported his parachute shredded by anti-aircraft fire. Carswell would not leave him, nor would the co-pilot, Lt. James L. O'Neal, of Maywood, Illinois; the other eight crewmen jumped. Without enough power to clear the mountains the plane crashed into a peak and exploded. Staff Sergeant Charlton S. Schnepf, of Hicksville, New York, the last man out, said just before he jumped he saw the bombardier kneeling on the flight deck beside Major Carswell and, "The major and O'Neal were just sitting there looking straight ahead."

Major Carswell received the Distinguished Flying Cross, the Air Medal, and was the first Fort Worther to receive the Congressional Medal of Honor. In 1948, Fort Worth Army Air Field became Carswell Air Force Base.

Fort Worth Army Air Field became Carswell Air Force Base in honor of Major
Horace A. Carswell, Jr., Fort Worth's first Congressional Medal of Honor winner.

Lucky Lady II Flew Non-stop Around the World

On February 26, 1949, an Air Force B-50, *Lucky Lady II*, left Carswell Air Force Base, heading eastward; 94 hours and one minute later she landed at Carswell after having completed the first non-stop flight around the world. *Lucky Lady II* had traveled 22,000 miles. The feat had been made possible through air-to-air-refueling by B-29 tankers at four places along the route. Air Force Secretary Stuart Symington said, "What this actually does is to turn our medium bombers into intercontinental bombers."

Round-the-world travel had interested man since Magellan's time. Stimulated by Jules Verne's *Around the World in Eighty Days*, Nellie Bly, a young reporter for Joseph Pulitzer's *New York World*, made the journey in 72 days, 6 hours, and 11 minutes by steamship and rail. The first air trip, in 1924, completed by two United States Army planes, required 175 days, of which only 14 days and 15 hours were spent in the air. The German *Graf Zepplin* cut the record to 21 days in August, 1929, and made Wiley Post believe he could circle the earth in ten days. Post and Harold Gatty actually made it in 8 days, 15 hours, and 51 minutes. Two years after the 1931 flight—and again using the *Winnie Mae*—Post was the first to fly around the world alone; his new record was 7 days, 18 hours and 49 ½ minutes. Howard Hughes, with several assistants, cut the record to 3 days, 19 hours and 8 minutes, in 1938.

Lucky Lady II, flown by first pilot Captain J. C. Gallagher and second pilot Arthur M. Neal, of the 8th Air Force, refueled over the Azores, Saudi Arabia, the Phillipines, and Hawaii. The Tucson-based, fourteen-man crew stood watches of six hours on and six hours off duty during the four days aloft. They slept in canvas hammocks slung from the bulkheads. Food was canned for the most part; the Air Force was trying out self-heating cans of spaghetti, soup, hamburgers, and boned chicken. To heat the contents it was only necessary to punch four holes in the bottom of the can, which triggered a warming chemical reaction.

Major General Roger Ramey, the commander of the 8th Air Force recommended all 14 crew members for the Distinguished Flying Cross.

Lucky Lady II, leaving Carswell Air Force Base and returning there, made the first non-stop flight around the world.

Rayburn Was Speaker Twice as Long as Henry Clay

Samuel Taliaferro Rayburn was born January 6, 1882, in the Clinch River country of Tennessee. When he was five he came with his parents and nine brothers and sisters to Fannin County. His Confederate father remained with Lee's army until the end and refused a captain's commission because he could then neither read nor write.

Rayburn's interest in politics came from hearing Congressman Joseph Weldon Bailey speak. Rayburn was about thirteen at the time. He finished his chores one morning, washed his feet at the pump, and headed for Bonham.

I remember it was a rainy day, and I made the several miles from our farm at Flag Springs on a mule over a gummy mud road to hear Bailey's magnificent speech, which he delivered in a covered "tabernacle" of the Evangelical Church. The place was jammed. It was raining and when I saw all those rich townfolk in store-bought clothes, I decided to stay outside. I found an open flap and listened for two hours. I can still feel the water dripping down my neck. I slipped around to the entrance when he was through, saw him come out, and followed him for five or six blocks until he got on a streetcar. Then I left, wondering whether I'd ever be as big a man as Joe Bailey.

Rayburn went home and announced that he would someday serve in the Congress.

When he was 17 Rayburn left the family's 40-acre farm to enroll in the Mayo Normal School at Commerce; he had $25 his father had given him. He got the job of ringing the bell that first year, climbing the tower each 45 minutes to signal the conclusion of classes and waiting five minutes to ring the beginning of the next ones. He was also the janitor at a public school and milked a cow for an old settler. He dropped out to teach; then, with his savings and working as a waiter and dishwasher, he graduated in 1903. Forty years later, as Speaker of the House of Representatives, he returned to the school, which was then East Texas State Teachers College, to receive the degree of Doctor of Laws.

After teaching at Dial and Lannius, Rayburn ran for the legislature in 1906 and won. Two years later he was admitted to the practice of law. As he began his third term, on January 10, 1911, he was elected Speaker of the Texas House; he was 29 years old. When his congressman did not seek re-election the following year, Rayburn bought a Model-T Ford and announced his candidacy. He defeated seven opponents with a 490-vote plurality of 21,336 cast in the Democratic primary, a victory which was the same as election since there were only 14 registered Republicans in Bonham and perhaps 200 in the entire district.

Congressman Rayburn began his service as Woodrow Wilson became president; other freshmen in the House included Alben W. Barkley, of Kentucky, who would later be Harry Truman's vice president. Fellow Texan John Nance Garner, who had already served ten years in the Congress, gave Rayburn help and advice; Garner would become Speaker of the House and Franklin Roosevelt's vice president. Speaker Champ Clark told Rayburn that he could attain a position of leadership if he were better educated and suggested that he read presidential biographies, which Rayburn termed "some of the best advice anyone ever gave me."

Bonham's Sam Rayburn was Speaker of the House longer than any other man.

Rayburn married Metze Jones of Valley View, Texas, the sister of Congressman Marvin Jones, on October 15, 1927, but the marriage lasted less than three months. He never discussed the marriage nor did he venture into matrimony again. Dwight Dorough, in his fine biography of Rayburn, noted that the Speaker regularly joked about his looks and that once when a photograph was sent to him to be signed he tore it up because, "If I permit a thing like that to be hung up in an office it will frighten off some old maid who might want to propose."

When John Nance Garner became speaker in 1931 Rayburn was one of his main lieutenants; John McCormack, of Massachusetts, was another. Rayburn supported Garner's 1932 presidential effort, although Franklin Roosevelt was the favorite. Roosevelt was nominated on the fourth ballot, with Garner his running mate.

In 1937 Rayburn became the majority leader. As Speaker William Bankhead's health declined, Rayburn assumed many of his public duties. War had begun in Europe and Roosevelt's second term was coming to an end. Rayburn hoped for a Garner nomination at the 1940 convention, but Roosevelt won with ease. A caucus of the Texas delegation, with Congressman Lyndon Johnson presiding, proposed Rayburn's nomination for the vice presidency, but Rayburn withdrew upon learning that Roosevelt preferred Henry A. Wallace. Speaker Bankhead died on September 15; on the following day Representative McCormack offered a resolution electing Sam Rayburn speaker, which passed unanimously.

On April 12, 1945, Rayburn set up a meeting with Vice President Harry Truman; he had a premonition that President Roosevelt was near death. Just before Truman arrived, a call came for him from the White House. When the Vice President arrived Rayburn said, "Harry, they said for you to call the White House." Truman returned the call, and presidential secretary Steve Early told him that Franklin Roosevelt had just died. Three days after taking the oath as president, Truman asked Rayburn's advice. Among other things, the Speaker warned of the president's staff:

> Some of them are not going to have too much ability . . . and some of them are not going to be able to stand up and battle it out with men of more ability than they've got, and they are going to try to do to you what they have tried to do to every president since I have been here. They are going to try to build a fence around you and in building that fence around you they will be keeping the very people away from seeing you that you should see.

In the 1946 election the Republicans gained control of the House. Rayburn's old friend from Massachusetts, Joe Martin, became the 45th speaker. Rayburn was the minority leader for the next two years. Democratic congressmen, realizing that the speaker's 1944 Cadillac was then in Republican Joe Martin's possession, bought a new 1947 black Cadillac for Rayburn. Since Rayburn was not much of a driver he had to hire his own chauffeur.

As a congressman Rayburn was able to take a greater part in debate than before. He had always supported legislation providing roads for farmers, rural electrification, school lunches, and soil conservation. As the Republicans began cutting appropriations for reclaiming farm land and preventing further damage he said:

> When I drive along the road or look out of the train window and see the fertile soil of the country washed down to rock bottom and gutted with ditches, it hurts me almost like the stick of a knife . . . . If we are the same kind of vandals for the next 25 years in the destruction of the fertility of our soil, we will not have any amount of surpluses to sell abroad, but we will be using every acre of this worn and torn land to raise the things that we have got to consume inside the United States of America.

Speaker Rayburn entertained the nation's leaders at his Bonham home.

The Truman whistle-stop campaign of 1948—in which Bonham was one of the stops—defeated Thomas E. Dewey and put the Democrats back into control of the House. Also, in that election Texas elected Rayburn's protege, Lyndon B. Johnson, to the Senate.

With a $10,000 award given by Colliers' magazine for distinguished service in government the Speaker announced plans for a library in Bonham. A few months thereafter a $50,000 donation was made by friends of Myron G. Blalock. By 1956, the library foundation had $200,000 and was ready to solicit bids for the building. Ground was broken in late 1955, and the library was opened October 9, 1957; it was of white Georgian marble and had cost half a million dollars.

On January 30, 1951, Rayburn broke Henry Clay's 125-year-old record of 3056½ days as speaker. For a day his fellow congressmen lauded him. Robert L. (Muley) Doughton, of North Carolina, the only congressman whose service then exceeded that of Rayburn, concluded his remarks with, "I cannot say so much for him as a father but he's still young, handsome, and popular. We still have hope for him in that respect." By 1953, when Joe Martin was again speaker by virtue of the Eisenhower victory, Minority Leader Rayburn was the oldest member of the House in point of service. Two years later he was again speaker and held that position for the rest of his life.

Sam Rayburn was the permanent chairman of the Democratic National Convention in 1948, 1952, and 1956. He refused to preside in 1960 because he wanted to try to get the presidential nomination for Lyndon Johnson. At Los Angeles, on July 13, he put Johnson's name in nomination, but the Kennedy forces were too well organized. When he returned to his room after Kennedy's nomination his phone rang; it was John Kennedy asking if he could come to his suite. When Rayburn arrived, Kennedy asked him to persuade Johnson to accept the vice presidential nomination.

Rayburn was in his 25th term and had doubled Clay's record as speaker when he was stricken with cancer. He returned to Bonham in August, 1961, spent October at Baylor Hospital in Dallas, then was taken back to Bonham, where he died November 16, 1961, at Joe Risser Hospital. The new speaker, John McCormack, named 105 members to represent the House at Rayburn's funeral. Among those in Bonham to pay their respects were President Harry Truman, President Dwight Eisenhower, President John Kennedy, and Vice President Lyndon Johnson.

Sam Rayburn served with eight presidents and well over 3,000 congressmen. He was speaker for 17 years and 2 months, almost twice as long as John McCormack's 8 years and 11 months and more than twice Henry Clay's 8 years and 4 months and Joe Cannon's 7 years and 4 months. His service in the Congress was 48 years and 8 months, which has been exceeded only by Carl Vinson's 50 years and 2 months, and Emanuel Celler's 49 years and 10 months.

Four presidents attended Sam Rayburn's Bonham funeral, including Harry Truman; John F. Kennedy, who would die seventy miles south of Bonham; Lyndon Johnson, who was born and would die in the hill country to the southwest; and Dwight Eisenhower, who was born thirty miles from Bonham.

The Sam Rayburn Library was established at Bonham during the Speaker's last years.

References

Books

Abernathy, John R. *In Camp with Theodore Roosevelt.* Oklahoma City: Times-Journal Publishing Company, 1933.

Barker, Eugene C., Editor. *A History of Texas and Texans.* Chicago and New York: The American Historical Society, 1914.

Barker, Eugene C. *The Life of Stephen F. Austin.* Austin: University of Texas Press, 1969.

Biesele, Rudolph Leopold. *The History of the German Settlements in Texas, 1831-1861.* Austin: Von Boeckmann-Jones Company, 1930.

Biggers, Don H. *German Pioneers in Texas.* Fredericksburg, Texas: Fredericksburg Publishing Company, 1925.

Bolton, H. E. *Texas in the Middle Eighteenth Century.* Austin: University of Texas Press, 1970.

Botkin, B. A., Editor. *Lay My Burden Down.* Chicago: University of Chicago Press, 1945.

Brown, John Henry. *Indian Wars and Pioneers of Texas.* Austin: L. E. Daniell, no date.

Brown, Ray Hyer. *Robert Stewart Hyer.* Salado, Texas: Anson Jones Press, 1957.

Carroll, James Milton. *A History of Texas Baptists.* Dallas: Baptist Standard Publishing Company, 1923.

Castañeda, Carlos E. *Our Catholic Heritage in Texas, 1519-1936.* Austin: Von Boeckmann-Jones Company, 1936.

Carter, R. G. *On the Border with Mackenzie.* New York: Antiquarian Press, Ltd., 1961.

Clark, James A. and Halbouty, Michael T. *The Last Boom.* New York: Random House, 1972.

Clark, James A. and Halbouty, Michael T. *Spindletop.* New York: Random House, 1952.

Coppini, Pompeo. *From Dawn to Sunset.* San Antonio: The Naylor Company, 1949.

Crocket, George. *Two Centuries in East Texas.* Dallas: The Southwest Press, 1932.

Davis, Britton. *The Truth About Geronimo.* New Haven: Yale University Press, 1929.

Dixon, Sam Houston. *The Men Who Made Texas Free.* Houston: Texas Historical Publishing Company, 1924.

Dorough, C. Dwight. *Mr. Sam.* New York: Random House, 1962.

Duganne, A. J. H. *Camps and Prisons, Twenty Months in the Department of the Gulf.* New York: J. P. Robens, 1865.

Duval, John C. *The Adventures of Big-Foot Wallace.* Philadelphia: Claxton, Remsen and Haffelfinger, 1871.

Eaves, Charles, and Hutchinson, C. A. *Post City, Texas.* Austin: The Texas State Historical Association, 1952.

Eby, Frederick. *The Development of Education in Texas.* New York: The Macmillan Company, 1925.

Elliott, Claude. *Leathercoat, the Life History of a Texas Patriot.* San Antonio: Standard Printing Company, 1938.

Emmett, Chris. *Texas Camel Tales.* San Antonio: The Naylor Company, 1932.

Frantz, Joe B. *Gail Borden, Dairyman to a Nation.* Norman: University of Oklahoma Press, 1951.

Friedrichs, Irene. *History of Goliad.* Victoria, Texas: Regal Printers, 1967.

Gard, Wayne. *Rawhide Texas.* Norman: University of Oklahoma Press, 1965.

Garrett, Julia. *Fort Worth: A Frontier Triumph.* Austin: Encino Press, 1972.

Geiser, Samuel Wood. *Naturalists of the Frontier.* Dallas: Southern Methodist University Press, 1948.

Gillespie County Historical Society. *Pioneers in God's Hills.* Austin: Von Boeckmann-Jones, 1960.

Good, Dennie D. *The Buffalo Soldier.* Tulsa: Gilcrease Institute, 1970.

Haas, Oscar. *History of New Braunfels and Comal County, Texas, 1844-1946.* Austin: Steck Company, 1968.

Haley, J. Evetts. *Charles Schreiner: General Merchandise.* Austin: Texas State Historical Association, 1944.

Handy, Mary Olivia. *The History of Fort Sam Houston.* San Antonio: The Naylor Company, 1951.

Henderson, Jeff S., Editor. *100 Years in Montague County.* Saint Jo, Texas: Ipta Printers, 1958.

Hilton, Conrad Nicholson. *Be My Guest.* Englewood Cliffs, New Jersey: Prentice Hall, Inc., 1957.

Hodge, Frederick Webb, editor. *Handbook of American Indians North of Mexico.* Smithsonian Institution Bureau of American Ethnology, Bulletin 30, Volume II, Washington, D. C.: U. S. Government Printing Office, 1910.

Hunter, J. Marvin. *Old Camp Verde, the Home of the Camels.* Bandera, Texas, 1962?

Inouye, Daniel and Elliott, Lawrence. *Journey to Washington.* Englewood Cliffs, New Jersey: Prentice Hall, Inc., 1967.

Jackson, Robert. *Living Lessons from the New London Explosion.* Nashville: The Parthenon Press, 1938.

Jackson, Robert. *The Remarkable Ride of the Abernathy Boys.* New York: Henry Z. Walck, Inc., 1967.

Johnson, Frank W. *A History of Texas and Texans*, Editor Eugene C. Barker. Chicago and New York: The American Historical Society, 1914.

Johnston, William Preston. *The Life of General Albert Sidney Johnston.* New York: D. Appleton and Company, 1879.

Kemp, L. W. *Signers of the Texas Declaration of Independence.* Houston: Anson Jones Press, 1944.

King, Irene Marschall. *John O. Meusebach, German Colonizer in Texas.* Austin: University of Texas Press, 1967.

Kirkland, Forrest, and Newcomb, W. W., Jr. *The Rock Art of Texas Indians.* Austin: University of Texas Press, 1967.

Klausen, C. A., Editor. *The Lady with the Pen, Elise Woerenskjold in Texas.* Northfield, Minnesota: Norwegian-American Historical Association, 1961.

Knight, Oliver. *Fort Worth, Outpost on the Trinity.* Norman: University of Oklahoma Press, 1953.

Kubiak, Daniel. *Monument to a Black Man.* San Antonio: The Naylor Company, 1972.

Leckie, William. *The Buffalo Soldiers.* Norman: University of Oklahoma Press, 1967.

Linn, John J. *Reminscences of Fifty Years in Texas.* Austin: The Steck Company, 1935.

Maguire, Jack, Editor. *A President's Country.* Austin: Alcalde Press, 1964.

McComb, David G. *Houston, The Bayou City.* Austin: University of Texas Press, 1969.

McConnell, H. H. *Five Years a Cavalryman.* Jacksboro, Texas: J. N. Rogers and Company, 1889.

McConnell, Joseph Carroll. *The West Texas Frontier.* Jacksboro, Texas: By the Author, Gazette Print, 1933.

McCullough, David. *The Great Bridge.* New York: Simon and Shuster, 1972.

McKay, Mrs. Arch and Spellings, Mrs. H. A. *A History of Jefferson, Marion County, 1836-1936*. Jefferson, 1936.

Memorial and Genealogical Record of Texas. Chicago: Goodspeed Brothers, 1894.

Mohler, Stanley R. and Johnson, Bobby H. *Wiley Post, His Winnie Mae and the World's First Pressure Suit*. Washington, D. C.: Smithsonian Institution Press, 1971.

Newcomb, W. W., Jr. *The Indians of Texas*. Austin: University of Texas Press, 1961.

Nye, W. S. *Carbine & Lance*. Norman: University of Oklahoma Press, 1969.

Olmsted, Frederick. *A Journey Through Texas*. New York: Dix, Edwards and Company, 1857.

Ormsby, Waterman L. *The Butterfield Overland Mail*. Lyle H. Wright and Josephine M. Bynum, editors. San Marino, California: The Huntington Library, 1942.

Paine, Albert Bigelow. *Captain Bill McDonald, Texas Ranger*. New York: J. J. Little and Ives Company, 1909.

Peak, Howard. *A Ranger of Commerce*. San Antonio: Naylor Printing Company, 1929.

Pioneers in God's Hills. Gillespie County Historical Society, editors. Austin: Von Boeckmann-Jones, 1960.

Pool, William C. *Bosque County, Texas*. San Marcos, Texas: San Marcos Record Press, 1954.

Post, Wiley and Gatty, Harold. *Around the World in Eight Days, the Flight of the Winnie Mae*. New York: Garden City Publishing Company, Inc., 1931.

Pray, Mrs. R. F. *Dick Dowling's Battle*. San Antonio: The Naylor Company, 1936.

Procter, Ben H. *Not Without Honor*. Austin: University of Texas Press, 1962.

Pryzygoda, Jacek. *Texas Pioneers from Poland*. Waco: Texian Press, 1971.

Rademaker, John A. *These are Americans*. Palo Alto, California: Pacific Books, 1951.

Reading, Robert S. *Arrows Over Texas*. San Antonio: The Naylor Company, 1960.

Reagan, John. *Memoirs*. New York and Washington: The Neale Publishing Company, 1906.

Rickenbacker, Edward V. *Rickenbacker*. Englewood Cliffs, New Jersey: Prentice Hall, Inc., 1967.

Rister, Carl. *Oil! Titan of the Southwest*. Norman: University of Oklahoma Press, 1949.

Roemer, Ferdinand. *Texas*. San Antonio: Stanton Printing Company, 1967.

Roosevelt, Theodore. *Outdoor Pastimes of an American Hunter*. New York: Charles Scribner's Sons, 1923.

Rourke, Constance. *Davy Crockett*. New York: Harcourt Brace and Company, 1934.

Santos, Richard G. *Letter From Columbia, Texas, December 27, 1836, addressed to Blas Herrera*. San Antonio: James W. Knight, 1966.

Scarbrough, Clara Stearns. *Land of Good Water*. Georgetown: Williamson County Sun, 1973.

Schoen, Harold, compiler. *Monuments Erected by the State of Texas to Commemorate the Centenary of Texas Independence*. Austin: Commission of Control for Texas Centennial Celebrations, 1938.

Shirey, Orville C. *Americans: The Story of the 442nd Combat Team*. Washington, D. C.: Infantry Journal Press, 1946.

Siegel, Stanley. *Big Men Walked Here*. Austin: The Pemberton Press, 1971.

Simmons, Lee. *Assignment Huntsville*. Austin: University of Texas Press, 1957.

Smith, Marie. *The President's Lady*. New York: Random House, 1964.

Sowell, A. J. *Life of Big-Foot Wallace*. Bandera, Texas: Frontier Times, 1899.

Stephens, I. K. *The Hermit Philosopher of Liendo*. Dallas: Southern Methodist University Press, 1951.

Stuck, Walter G. *José Francisco Ruíz, Texas Patriot*. San Antonio: Witte Memorial Museum, 1963.

Taft, Lorado. *The History of American Sculpture*. New York: The Macmillan Company, 1903.

Tatum, Lawrie. *Our Red Brothers and the Peace Policy of President Ulysses S. Grant*. Lincoln, Nebraska: University of Nebraska Press, 1970.

Taylor, Mrs. Bride Neill. *Elisabet Ney, Sculptor*. Austin: By the Author, 1938.

Thrall, Homer S. *A Brief History of Methodism in Texas*. Nashville, Tennessee: Publishing House of the Methodist Church, 1894.

Toepperwein, Herman. *Nimitz: Steamboat Hotel*. Fredericksburg, Texas: The Admiral Nimitz Foundation, 1972.

Vestal, Stanley. *Bigfoot Wallace*. Boston: Houghton Mifflin Company, 1942.

Wallace, Ernest and Vigness, David M., Editors. *Documents of Texas History, Vol. I*. Lubbock: Texas Technological College, 1960.

Warner, C. A. *Texas Oil and Gas Since 1543*. Houston: Gulf Publishing Company, 1939.

Webb, Walter Prescott, editor. *The Handbook of Texas.* Austin: The Texas State Historical Association, 1952.

Weddle, Robert S. *The San Sabá Mission.* Austin: University of Texas Press, 1964.

White, Michael A. *The History of Baylor University, 1845-1861.* Waco: Texian Press, 1968.

Wilbarger, J. W. *Indian Depredations in Texas.* Austin: The Steck Company, 1935.

Williams, Amelia W. and Barker, Eugene C., Editors. *The Writings of Sam Houston, 1813-1863, Volumes III and IV.* Austin: Jenkins Publishing Company, 1970.

Winfrey, Dorman. *A History of Rusk County, Texas.* Waco: Texian Press, 1961.

Winfrey, Dorman. *Along the Early Trails of the Southwest.* Austin: Jenkins Publishing Company, 1969.

Special Publications

Biographical Sketch of Conrad Hilton. Hilton Hotels Corporation. 1973.

Blake, R. B. *Historic Nacogdoches.* Nacogdoches: Red Lamp Herald, 1939.

Chester W. Nimitz. The Admiral Nimitz Foundation, Fredericksburg, 1971.

Congressional Record, March 9, 1967.

Elisabet Ney Museum, Austin Parks and Recreation Department Information Bureau.

57th Annual Report of the Commissioner of Indian Affairs. Washington, D.C.: U.S. Government Printing Office, 1888.

Daniel, Theo S., Chairman, Henderson County Historical Survey Committee, *Malakoff Man,* a news release, 1969.

Farrar, R. N. *The Story of Buffalo Bayou and the Houston Ship Channel.* Houston: The Houston Chamber of Commerce, 1926.

General Foods Family Album, General Foods Corporation, 1948.

1972 Annual Report, General Foods Corporation.

Sellards, E. H. *Old Man Malakoff, a Prehistoric Stone Image.* Information Circular No. 18, Austin: Texas Memorial Museum, 1940.

Welcome to Fort Concho. San Angelo: Fort Concho Museum.

Woolford, Bess Carrol and Quillin, Ellen Schulz. *The Story of the Witte Museum, 1922-1960.*

Magazines

Andrews, Myrtle. "Yesterdays," *New Mexico*, (April, 1937).

Barker, Eugene C., Editor. "Journal of Stephen F. Austin," *Quarterly of the Texas State Historical Association, VII*, (April, 1904), p. 288.

Burke, Admiral Arleigh. "Admiral Chester Nimitz, RIP," *National Review*, (May 22, 1966).

Bragg, J. D. "Waco University," *Southwestern Historical Quarterly, Volume LI*, (January, 1949), pp. 213-224.

Conger, Roger. "The Waco Suspension Bridge," *Texana*, (Summer, 1963).

"Crockett, Mrs. Elizabeth," *The Cattleman*, (November, 1952).

Friend, Llerena. "Old Spanish Fort," *The West Texas Historical Association Yearbook*, (1940).

Goetz, Otto. "The Painted Rocks of Concho County, Texas, a Forgotten National Monument," *West Texas Historical Association Yearbook*, (1940).

Goode, Monroe. "John R. Abernathy—Wolfer Extraordinary," *The Cattleman*, (January, 1940).

Hollon, Gene. "Captain Charles Schreiner, the Father of the Hill Country," *The Southwestern Historical Quarterly, Vol. XLVIII*, (October, 1944).

McCormack, John F., Jr. "Sabine Pass." *Civil War Times Illustrated*, (December, 1973).

Muir, Andrew. "The Texas State Cemetery," *Texas Parade*, (September, 1950).

Murray, Myrtle. "Home Life on the Early Ranches of Southwest Texas, Chapter XII," *The Cattleman*, (December, 1938).

Richardson, Rupert N. "Some Details of the Southern Overland Mail," *Southwestern Historical Quarterly, Vol. XXIX, No. 1*, (July, 1925), pp. 1-18.

Rippy, J. Fred. "Border Troubles Along the Rio Grande, 1848-1860," *Southwestern Historical Quarterly, Vol. XXIII, No. 2*, (October, 1919), pp. 91-111.

Sellards, E. H. "Stone Images from Henderson County, Texas," *American Antiquity, Vol. VII, No. 1*, (1941), pp. 29-38.

Strickland, Rex W. "History of Fannin County, 1836-1843," *Southwestern Historical Quarterly*, (July, 1930).

Newspapers

Abilene Reporter-News, February 28, 1967.

Athens Review, February 20, 1930; August 12, 1967; April 28, 1970.

Bonham Daily Favorite, October 8, 1957.

Carswell Air Force Base Aerospace Sentinel, March 17, 1972.

Dallas Morning News, February 21, 1900; January 2, 5, 6, 7, 1922; January 5, 1951; April 6, 1972; October 8, 1972; July 24, and October 1, 1973.

Fort Worth Star Telegram, July 17-23, 1933; August 8-18, 1935; March 18, 19, 20, 21, 22, 25, 26, 1937; November 24, 1944; August 26, 1945; March 3, 1948; March 4-6, 1949; May 30, 1951.

The Fredericksburg Radio-Post, April 19, 1962.

Kilgore News Herald, March 17, 1972

Malakoff News, February 29, 1930; August 12, 18, 1967; February 6, 1970.

Nacogdoches Sunday Sentinel, Geneva Stephens article. April 7, 1974.

Pioneer News-Observer, Kerrville, February, 1974.

The Port Arthur News, March 17, 1972.

The Potosi Journal, April 20 and May 4, 1904.

The Potosi Independent-Journal, April 28 and June 2, 1938; February 3, 1949; January 18, 1962; August 8, 1968.

The San Antonio Light, September 16 and October 22, 1886.

The St. Louis Post-Dispatch, April 21, 22, 26, and May 8, 1938; February 2, 1949.

Unpublished Manuscripts

Allen, Winnie. "The History of Nacogdoches, 1691-1830." M. A. thesis, University of Texas at Austin, 1925.

Barrett, Arrie. "Federal Military Outposts in Texas, 1846-1861" M. A. thesis, University of Texas at Austin, 1927.

Beam, Harold. "A History of Collin County, Texas" M. A. thesis, University of Texas at Austin, 1951.

Boggs, Herschel. "The History of Fort Concho" M. A. thesis, University of Texas at Austin, 1940.

Curtis, Sarah K. "A History of Gillespie County, Texas, 1846-1900" M. A. thesis, University of Texas at Austin, 1943.

Donnell, Guy. "The History of Montague County, Texas" M. A. thesis, University of Texas at Austin, 1940.

Franklin, Nancy Dillard. "The History of Mexia, Texas" M. A. thesis, Southern Methodist University 1966.

Good, Benjamin. "John Henninger Reagan," Ph. D. dissertation, University of Texas at Austin, 1932.

Grusendorf, Arthur Robert. "The Social and Philosophical Determinants of Education in Washington County" Ph. D. dissertation, University of Texas at Austin, 1938.

Hendricks, Delia Ann. "The History of Cattle and Oil in Tarrant County" M. A. thesis, Texas Christian University, 1969.

Holbert, Ruby Crawford. "The Public Career of James Webb Throckmorton" M. A. thesis, University of Texas at Austin, 1932.

Jenschke, Joan. "Churches in Fredericksburg," 1974.

Lee, Lois Carol. "Goliad County: A General Study of its History" M. A. thesis, Texas Christian University, 1959.

Ledlow, William Franklin. "History of Protestant Education, A Study of the Origin, Growth, and Development of Education Endeavors in Texas" Ph. D. dissertation, University of Texas at Austin, 1926.

McCullough, Mary. "The Butterfield Overland Mail Company," 1972.

Martin, Everette Armstrong. "A History of the Sprindletop Oil Field" M. A. thesis, University of Texas at Austin, 1934.

Meyers, Mary. "Lifting the Grave," 1972.

Orchard, Elizabeth. "The History of the Development of Fort Sam Houston" M.A. thesis, University of Texas at Austin, 1937.

Prince, Diane E. "William Goyens, Free Negro on the Texas Frontier" M. A. thesis, Stephen F. Austin State College, 1967.

Reddell, Clara McKinney. "Collin McKinney," 1971.

Roark, Mrs. Garland. "Old Nacogdoches University Building," 1964.

Tatum, Bowen C. "The Penitentiary Movement in Texas, 1847-1849" M. A. thesis, Sam Houston State University, 1970.

Tidwell, D. D., "A History of the West Fork Baptist Association" Ph. D. dissertation, Southwestern Baptist Theological Seminary, 1940.

Wangler, Kay. "The History of Birdville," 1972.

Watson, Judy. "Jefferson, Texas: The Rise and Decline of the Cypress Port, 1842-1873" M. A. thesis, Texas Christian University, 1967.

Williams, J. W. "The Marcy and the Butterfield Trails Across North Texas" M. A. thesis, Hardin-Simmons University, 1933.

Interviews

Abernathy, Louie Van, Wichita Falls, Texas. Interview with author, July 21, 1973
Roach, Chris, Paint Rock, Texas. Interview with author, March 21, 1974.
Showalter, George. Potosi, Missouri. Interview with Mary Meyers.

Letters

Beckham, Clara. Athens, Texas. Letter to author, May 17, 1972.

Bennett, Charles, Member of Congress. Washington, D. C. Letter to author, May 16, 1974.

Brown, Artis, Columbus, Ohio. Letter to author, January 18, 1974.

Jennings, Mrs. Arthur. Texarkana, Texas. Letter to author, August 24, 1973.

Martin, Mrs. H. R. Mexia, Texas. Letter to author, March 1, 1974.

Maynard, Mrs. W. E. Bastrop, Texas. Letter to author, April 15, 1974.

Pace, Rankin. Winters, Texas. Letter to author, August 25, 1973.

Peacock, Laura. Jacksboro, Texas. Letter to author, November 27, 1973.

Pirkey, Mrs. Earl. DeKalb, Texas. Letter to author, August 28, 1973.

Reierson, Ole. Brownsboro, Texas. Letter to H. Johnson, Holt, Norway, May 28, 1849.

Robinson, Ella. Meridian, Texas. Letter to author, October 30, 1972.

Taliaferro, J. C. Sherman, Texas. Letter to author, April 30, 1974.

Whisenant, Ernest. Brownsboro, Texas. Letter to author, April 27, 1972.

Maps

Coursey, Clark. *Courthouses of Texas*. Brownwood: Banner Printing Co., 1962.

Notes

1. Indians painted. . . .Roach, Goetz, Kirkland and Newcomb.

2. Spanish Fort was. . . .Hodge, Henderson, McConnell 1933, Donnell, Friend.

3. The Taovaya Village flew. . . .Hodge, McConnell 1933, Donnell, Friend, Bolton, Weddle.

4. William Goyens was. . . .Prince, Blake, Kubiak, Barker 1969, Barker 1965.

5. Josiah Wilbarger was. . . .Wilbarger, Maynard.

6. José Ruíz signed. . . .Stuck, Woolford and Quillin, Dixon.

7. McKinney was. . . .Siegel, Linn, Reddell, Beam, Kemp.

8. Francisco Ruíz was. . . .Woolford and Quillen, Santos, Castañeda.

9. Johanna Troutman designed. . . .Webb.

10. Gail Borden laid out. . . .Frantz, Brown, Olmsted.

11. Johnston dueled. . . .Johnston.

12. Bigfoot Wallace was. . . .Sowell, Duval, Vestal.

13. The Ship Channel made. . . .Farrar, McComb, Peck.

14. John B. Denton was. . . .Strickland, Knight, Garrett, Wangler.

15. Houston signed. . . .Johnson, Garrett, Williams and Barker, Wallace and Vigness.

16 Jefferson was. . . .Watson, Barker 1914, McKay and Spellings.

17. The Dalby Springs Congregation has met. . . .Jennings, Pirkey.

18. The Round Rock marked. . . .Scarbrough.

19. Baylor opened. . . .Carroll, Grusendorf, Bragg, White.

20. Nacogdoches University was. . . .Blake, Allen, Rourke, *Dallas Morning News*, *Nacogdoches Sentinel*.

21. Southwestern's predecessors were. . . .Brown 1957, *Dallas Morning News*, Eby, Crocket.

22. Prince Carl founded. . . .King, Curtis, Haas.

23. John O. Meusebach founded. . . .King, Curtis, Biggers, Haas, Gillespie County Historical Society.

24. The Adelsverein built. . . .Biesele, Biggers, Curtis.

25. A Cross stands . . . . Biggers, King, Maguire, Gillespie County Historical Society, *Fredericksburg Radio-Post*.

26. The Nimitz was. . . .Biggers, King, Toepperwein.

27. Norwegians settled. . . .Pool, Klausen, Reierson, Beckham, Whisenant.

28. A Norwegian lady wrote. . . .Klausen.

29. The penitentiary was located. . . .Tatum, Simmons, Duganne.

30. A fort was. . . .Garrett, Tidwell, Barrett, Knight.

31. Lindheimer was. . . .Haas, Biesele, Roemer, Geiser.

32. A cemetery was. . . .Johnston, Muir.

33. Elizabeth Crockett followed. . . .*The Cattleman*, Rourke.

34. Panna Maria was. . . .Barker 1914, Pryzygoda.

35. The Camels were. . . .Barrett, Emmett, Rister 1946, Hunter.

36. Goliad has. . . .Martin 1937, Lee, Rippy, Friedrichs.

37. Charles Schreiner settled. . . .Haley, Hollon, Murray.

38. Ormsby rode. . . .Richardson, Winfrey 1969, Williams, Ormsby, McCullough.

39. John Reagan was. . . .Procter, Reagan, Gard, Good.

40. Dick Dowling turned. . . .Pray, Duganne, *Pioneer News-Observer*, McCormack.

41. James Throckmorton was. . . .Elliott, Holbert, Beam.

42. Peter Robinson bought. . . .Botkin, Robinson.

43. A Fort was. . . .Boggs, Fort Concho bulletin, Leckie, Carter, Good.

44. Fort Richardson was. . . .McConnell 1889, Carter.

45. Satanta was. . . .McConnell 1889, Carter, Tatum, Nye.

46. Waco bridged. . . .Conger, D. McCullough 1972.

47. Fort Sam was. . . .Handy, Orchard.

48. Geronimo was. . . .*San Antonio Light*, Hodge, Handy, *57th Annual Report of the Commissioner of Indian Affairs*, Orchard.

49. Oil Springs was. . . .Warren, Rister 1949.

50. Elisabet Ney sculpted. . . .Stephens, Taylor, Taft.

51. Corsicana was. . . .Warren, Rister 1949.

52. The Twentieth Century came in. . . .Martin, Rister 1949, Clark and Halbouty 1952, Warren.

53. Fort Worth became. . . .Hendricks, Knight.

54. The Stockyards were. . . .Hendricks, Knight.

55. Theodore Roosevelt came to. . . .Abernathy 1933, Roosevelt, Goode, Taliaferro, Paine.

56. Jack Abernathy caught. . . .Abernathy 1933,1973, Roosevelt, Goode, Paine.

57. The Abernathy boys rode. . . .Jackson, Abernathy 1973.

58. Charles Post changed. . . .*General Foods Family Album*, *General Foods 1972 Annual Report*, Eaves and Hutchinson.

59. Eddie Rickenbacker was. . . .Rickenbacker, *Dallas Morning News*.

60. Gus Noyes raised. . . .Coppini, *Abilene Reporter-News*, Pace.

61. John Pershing came. . . .Franklin, Martin 1974, *Dallas Morning News*, Rister 1949.

62. The Mobley was. . . .Andrews, Hilton 1957, 1973.

63. The Malakoff heads were. . . .Sellards 1940, 1941, Daniel, Newcomb, *Malakoff News*, *Athens Review*.

64. Wiley Post flew. . . .Post and Gatty, Mohler and Johnson, *Fort Worth Star-Telegram*.

65. A Generation died. . . .Clark and Halbouty 1972, *Fort Worth Star-Telegram*, Jackson 1933, *Port Arthur News*, *Kilgore News Herald*, Winfrey 1961.

66. Texans tried. . . .Barker, Meyers, *Potosi Journal*, *St. Louis Post-Dispatch*.

67. Claudia Taylor became. . . .Smith.

68. Nimitz accepted. . . .Brown, Burke, Nimitz.

69. Inouye became. . . .Inouye, Shirey, Rademaker.

70. Major Carswell sank. . . .*Fort Worth Star-Telegram*.

71. Carswell fliers flew. . . .*Fort Worth Star-Telegram*.

72. Rayburn was. . . .Dorough, Bennett, *Congressional Record*.

In addition, Webb was consulted regularly.

INDEX